Arizona's Hispanic Flyboys 1941-1945

Arizona's Hispanic Flyboys 1941-1945

Rudolph C. Villarreal

Writers Club Press
New York Lincoln Shanghai

Arizona's Hispanic Flyboys 1941-1945

All Rights Reserved © 2002 by Rudolph Colomo Villarreal

No part of this book may be reproduced or transmitted in any form or by any means, graphic, electronic, or mechanical, including photocopying, recording, taping, or by any information storage retrieval system, without the written permission of the publisher.

Writers Club Press
an imprint of iUniverse, Inc.

For information address:
iUniverse, Inc.
2021 Pine Lake Road, Suite 100
Lincoln, NE 68512
www.iuniverse.com

ISBN: 0-595-25717-8 (pbk)
ISBN: 0-595-65280-8 (cloth)

Printed in the United States of America

To those referred to by Tom Brokaw as "The Greatest Generation".

Contents

Introduction 1
STAFF SERGEANT ERNEST P. ABRIL 5
STAFF SERGEANT NORMAN F. ACIDO 7
FIRST LIEUTENANT MANUEL AGUIRRE 9
STAFF SERGEANT ERNEST T. ALVAREZ 13
STAFF SERGEANT DAVID S. AVILA 15
LIEUTENANT APOLONIO (HAP) BARRAZA 17
STAFF SERGEANT FERNANDO (FRITZ) BELIS 21
TECHNICAL SERGEANT RAYMOND BERNAL 23
STAFF SERGEANT AMADO BERRELLEZ 25
STAFF SERGEANT INOCENTE (CHENTE) R.
    BOLTAREZ 27
STAFF SERGEANT EPIFANIO (EPPY) P. CAMPOS 31
TECHNICAL SERGEANT SERVANDO B. CARRILLO 33
LIEUTENANT IGNACIO (NASH) CASTRO 35
STAFF SERGEANT VICTOR V. CERVANTEZ 39
TECH SERGEANT FRANCISCO J. COLUNGA 41
SERGEANT GUSTAVO E. CONTRERAS 43
CAPTAIN LUIS BONILLAS COPPOLA 45

LIEUTENANT VALDEMAR A. CORDOVA 49
TECHNICAL SERGEANT GILBERT S. CORONA. 53
FIRST LIEUTENANT VIDAL J. CORTEZ 55
LIEUTENANT HECTOR E. DEVARGAS 59
FLIGHT OFFICER BENJAMIN DIAZ 63
STAFF SERGEANT JULIO R. DIAZ..................... 65
CAPTAIN JOSEPH S. DOMINGUEZ 69
SERGEANT ARTHUR R. ESTRADA 71
CORPORAL OSCAR C. GALLEGOS 73
FIRST LIEUTENANT EDWARD A. GARCIA 75
CAPTAIN ROBERT M. GARCIA 79
FIRST LIEUTENANT GILBERT F. GONZALES 83
STAFF SERGEANT NICOLAS B. GUERRA. 87
STAFF SERGEANT ALFRED L. HUISH JR 91
LIEUTENANT HEBER M. HUISH 93
STAFF SERGEANT MANUEL H. LARINI................. 95
SERGEANT HENRY L. LEYVA. 99
FIRST LIEUTENANT ORLANDO LOERA 101
STAFF SERGEANT FRANK G. MABANTE................ 103
STAFF SERGEANT JAMES A. MABANTE. 109
FLIGHT OFFICER JUAN S. MADERO 111
ARM2/c ALBERT E. MADRID 113
WARRANT OFFICER EUGENE A. MARIN 115
ENSIGN ALFRED C. MARQUEZ 117

FIRST LIEUTENANT RALPH LOUIS MICHELENA 119

CAPTAIN RAYMOND N. MORAGA 123

LIEUTENANT RAYMOND B. MORALES 131

TECHNICAL SERGEANT CHARLES P. NAVARRO 135

TECHNICAL SERGEANT RAUL A. NEGRETTE 137

STAFF SERGEANT MANUEL W. NEVARES 141

STAFF SERGEANT FRANK M. OCHOA 143

FLIGHT OFFICER REYES L. OLACHEA 145

STAFF SERGEANT RUDY L. OLAGUE 147

TECHNICAL SERGEANT GREGORIO OLIVA 149

FIRST LIEUTENANT GILBERT DURAN ORRANTIA 151

TECHNICAL SERGEANT ALFONSO M. ORTEGA 155

FIRST LIEUTENANT JOSE V. ORTEGA 159

SERGEANT JOE B. PACHECO 161

CORPORAL RICHARD S. PEYRON 163

LIEUTENANT ALPHONSE D. QUINONES 165

STAFF SERGEANT MANUEL A. RAMIREZ 173

STAFF SERGEANT MANUEL M. RAMOS 175

SERGEANT MIGUEL A. REYES 177

AMM2 EVERARDO R. REYNOSO 179

STAFF SERGEANT JOE P. RUIZ 181

SERGEANT JESUS M. SALAS 183

STAFF SERGEANT ALBERT M. SALAZAR 185

TECHNICAL SERGEANT ROBERT L. SANCHEZ 187

FIRST LIEUTENANT HECTOR J. SANTA ANNA 191
SERGEANT FRED C. SAUCEDO. 197
FIRST LIEUTENANT MIGUEL M. SERNA 199
LIEUTENANT ROBERT S. SOSA 203
STAFF SERGEANT CHARLES M. SOTELO 205
CAPTAIN OSCAR C. SOTO 207
FIRST LIEUTENANT MANUEL J. TREVINO JR. 209
TECHNICAL SERGEANT JOHN R. TRUJILLO 213
CAPTAIN ROGER E. VARGAS. 217
STAFF SERGEANT RAUL VASQUEZ 221
ARM1c JOHN L. VILLARREAL 223
STAFF SERGEANT JOE YANEZ 229
Appendix A ACRONYMS AND ABBREVIATIONS 231
Appendix B FLYBOY LIST 233
Bibliography. 245
About the Author 249

ACKNOWLEDGEMENTS

I would like to thank my wife Mary Ellen and daughter Lynn Rene, for typing the early drafts, and to Erik Ludwig, for his welcomed comments in editing the completed manuscript. To my nephew David, for his impressive cover design, and to my son Steve, for his computer assistance, I am also thankful.

This book could not have been written without the military records, photographs, and other information provided by those veteran airmen or their surviving family members. To them, I am deeply grateful.

Introduction

Over a half-century has passed since we Americans were involved in a monumental world conflict, the Second World War. During those years the world was not a friendly place. Pain, death and destruction were everywhere, especially in Europe, Asia, Africa and the South Pacific. From 1941 to late 1945, newspapers were full of the effects of this war. Accounts of major and minor battles, troop landings, invasions, ships sunk, planes destroyed, and casualty lists, were a daily part of the news.

During the war my father, Rodolfo R. Villarreal, was a civil service employee at the US Naval Air Station on North Island in San Diego, California. Although I was only four or five years old at the time, I remember the nighttime lighting restrictions and the victory garden where we lived at 2252 Grand Avenue in Pacific Beach. I can recall the camouflaged exterior walls at the Consolidated Aircraft factory where war planes were being built, tokens and stamps used to purchase rationed food items and gasoline, masking tape dimming the headlights of my father's automobile, and swarms of men and women everywhere in uniform. Perhaps it was all the activity witnessed on the home front of this busy port city that sparked my lifelong interest in learning what had happened overseas.

World War II remains one of the most significant historical events of the 20th century. It has been well documented in print and film over the last sixty years. Not much, however, has been written about Hispanics who served in uniform from 1941 through 1945. This is especially true of those who served in the so-called "glamorous" air corps of the US Army and Navy.

This is a documentary of Hispanic boys from my home state of Arizona who served as pilots and aircrew in our armed forces during the war. "Boys" is probably not a good choice of words, since some were already men in their mid-twenties. "Boys", however, could be applied to those who were still in their teens. And there were many.

I do not wish to give the impression that Hispanics were a large percentage of pilots and aircrews. They were, in fact, a small minority, even when taken together with other ethnic minorities from Arizona such as Italians, Chinese, Greek, Serbian, and Native Americans. Anglos made up the majority of those serving in the American armed forces, and the Air Corps was similarly comprised.

I have documented the experiences of Arizona Hispanics who served as pilots, navigators, bombardiers, flight engineers, gunners, and radio operators. My primary sources for locating the names of these individuals were the wartime newspapers from towns and cities throughout Arizona. From a compiled list (see appendix) of almost two hundred names, I was able to obtain additional information from submitted questionnaires, Missing Aircrew Reports, books, newspaper items, and other sources. The seventy-seven airmen included in the text of the book are featured alphabetically with name/rank, hometown, service information, combat decorations, experiences and a biographical sketch of their life after the war.

As already stated, wartime newspapers were the main source for compiling the list of pilots and aircrew. This listing is undoubtedly incomplete. I regret omission of any airmen who should be listed. With over fifteen million Americans in uniform during the war, the printed media faced an awesome challenge in attempting to cover all news concerning their hometown men and women in the armed forces. Very likely, some names didn't show up in print for me to retrieve years later. Another potential cause for omissions is that not all Hispanics have Spanish surnames. Hispanics make up a diverse group of ethnicities. There has been, for hundreds of years, a mixing of many nationalities in Mexico and the American Southwest. It is not surprising to find Hispanics with surnames of English, Irish, German, French, Italian, or Arabic origin. While researching the newspapers, it's not likely I would have known Heber Huish, Salvador Jury or Luis Coppola were part Hispanic without that information having been given to me by someone who knew them. It is not possible to know how many more names might have been included.

It is interesting to note that the highest rank attained during the war by anyone listed here was captain in the Army Air Corps and its equivalent rank of lieutenant in the US Navy. Why was higher rank not achieved? First, none were professional soldiers or sailors. In fact, there had never been a Hispanic from Arizona appointed to either West Point or Annapolis until after the war (The Air Force academy was founded in 1954). None had received reserve commissions through college ROTC, and thus there was less opportunity to acquire the necessary leadership skills. However, a few did complete college prior to entering the service: Roger Vargas graduated from Northern Arizona State Teachers College (now NAU) in 1939; Edward Garcia graduated from the University Of Arizona in 1941; Orlando Loera and Robert Sosa both graduated from Arizona State Teachers College (now ASU) respectively in 1941 and 1942. Sadly, both Loera and Sosa were killed while serving in Europe. These were all "citizen soldiers", most of whom had volunteered for the Army and Navy air services after our entry into the war. Racism may have been another factor which kept some men from achieving higher rank, it being no secret that blatant discrimination still existed at that time. It's ironic and sad that Raymond Moraga, a fighter pilot killed during the invasion of France in June 1944, never knew that his younger siblings would one day be allowed to swim with Anglos in the public pool in their hometown of Tempe.

With the termination of hostilities in 1945, many Hispanic servicemen returning home began to take advantage of the educational opportunities offered by the GI Bill of Rights. Two veteran pilots, Valdemar Cordova and Alfred Marquez, became attorneys and eventually Federal District Court Judges. Mr. Cordova began serving on the Federal bench in Phoenix in 1979, and Mr. Marquez in Tucson in 1980.

Some chose careers in education as schoolteachers, college professors and administrators. Others became entrepreneurs and successfully ran their own businesses in various industries. Not everyone elected to return to civilian life when the war ended. Several remained in the military and a few served during the Korean War and the Vietnam War as well. Six achieved the rank of lieutenant colonel during their Air Force careers.

Hispanics make up the largest ethnic minority in Arizona. Many of Arizona's Hispanics served valiantly in ground and sea forces during World War II, and today, in the Hispanic community as elsewhere, their service is remembered proudly. Less well known, however, is the contribution made by Arizona Hispanics in the elite volunteer services that fought the war from above.

It is my hope that this documentary serves as a tribute to and acknowledgement of those young Hispanic Arizonans who answered the call when their country needed them most.

Rudolph C. Villarreal

STAFF SERGEANT ERNEST P. ABRIL

TUCSON

Army Air Corps
Entered Service 1942
Gunner on B-24 "Pappy's Chillun", and B-17
835th Bomb Squadron, 486th Bomb Group
European Theater, 8th Air Force
Decorations Unknown

Ernest completed training at airfields in Colorado, Idaho, Texas, and Davis-Monthan Field in Tucson, Arizona. In the spring of 1944 he flew with his unit, the 486th Bomb Group, to Brazil, North Africa and finally to Sudbury, England about fifty miles NE of London. In April 1944, Sgt. Abril flew his first mission to bomb targets on the European continent and by October of that year had completed 30 missions.[1] Returning home he married the former Carmelita Garcia of Tucson in April 1945. The marriage didn't last and they were divorced 15 months later. They had one child.

Carmelita remembers one wartime experience that Ernest related to her. On one mission, while his bomber was under attack from a German fighter plane, he came face to face with the enemy pilot, and for a

---

1. To learn more of "Pappy's Chillun", the 835th Bomb Squadron, and the 486th Bomb Group, go to the following Web site on the Internet. www.486th.org

brief moment their eyes made contact but neither man fired his weapon. When asked why, he said he didn't know.

In October 1950, Mr. Abril died in an automobile accident. He was 26 years old.

STAFF SERGEANT
NORMAN F. ACIDO

NOGALES

Army Air Corps
Gunner on B-24 H
715th Bomb Squadron, 448th Bomb Group
European Theater, 8th Air Force
Air Medal

Sergeant Acido, ball turret gunner on a B-24 Liberator, was killed on January 5, 1944 when his plane was shot down on a mission to Kiel Germany from his base at Seething, England.[1] He was 22 years old and a graduate of Nogales High School class of 1940.

---

1. Missing Aircrew Report #2515, National Archives, Suitland, Maryland.

FIRST LIEUTENANT MANUEL AGUIRRE

MORENCI

Army Air Corps
Entered Service in August 1941
Bombardier on B-24 "Lakanooky"
783rd Bomb Squadron, 465th Bomb Group
Mediterranean Theater, 15th Air Force
Air Medal with 2 OLC

Manuel graduated from Morenci High School in May of 1941 and soon after enlisted in the Army Air Corps. By December of that year he was stationed at Hickam Field, Hawaii. When the Japanese attacked Pearl Harbor on December 7, Manuel found himself dodging bullets and bombs while attempting to bring down low flying enemy planes with his rifle.

Returning to the States, Manuel was sent to Las Vegas, Nevada for aerial gunnery school, which he completed in October 1942. Later, with the increasing need for flying officers to crew medium and heavy bombers, Manuel applied for and was accepted for bombardier training. In July 1944 Cadet Aguirre was presented his silver wings and commissioned a second lieutenant at Victorville army airfield in California.

Assigned to the Mediterranean Theater, Manuel began flying combat missions from Canosa, his base in Southern Italy. He flew his first mission on December 16, 1944 against the heavily defended oil refineries in Brux, Germany. Total flight time was seven hours and forty-five minutes and was typical of his first fifteen missions flown. Carrying loads of eight five-hundred-pound bombs on each B-24 Liberator, their targets were facilities of strategic importance such as war materials factories and transportation hubs. By this late period in the war, the Allies had secured control of the air and were seldom challenged by enemy fighter planes.

A greater threat to American flyers, however, was the accurate and intense anti-aircraft fire (flak) located at these targets. In addition to Brux, other difficult missions were to Vienna and Linz, Austria; Prague, Czechoslovakia; Regensburg and Augsburg, Germany. Most of Manuel's last ten missions were against tactical targets, such as bridges and troop movements behind enemy lines in support of the U.S. 5th Army in the Bologna, Italy area.

Lt. Manuel Aguirre and combat crew during training at Tonopah, Nevada October 1944. Manuel is standing at far left.[1]

With the war in Europe over, Manuel returned to the States in June 1945 and was separated from the service in November of that year. He returned to Arizona with the intention of attending the University of Arizona under the GI Bill. However, not long after arriving in Morenci, a visiting Army recruiting sergeant offered him the rank of master sergeant based on his prior service as an officer. Accepting the offer, his new duty assignment was in Panama as he had requested. When the Korean War began, he applied for recall to active duty as a bombardier in his reserve grade of first lieutenant. This was approved and in September of 1950, he reported to Randolph Field, Texas, where he trained B-29 bomber crews until 1953. Deciding to make the Air Force his career he applied for high-speed navigation training and upon completion was assigned to the Strategic Air Command as navigator in the Boeing B-47 Stratojet. He remained with SAC until retirement in 1964 with the rank of major. His decorations include the Air Medal with 2 OLC, Air Force Commendation Medal, National

---

1. All photos courtesy of Manuel Aguirre.

Defense Service Medal, WWII Victory Medal, combat ribbons for service in the European Theater and the Pacific Theater (WWII), and Outstanding Unit Award (310th Bomb Wing in SAC).

Moving to Orlando, Florida with his wife and two children, he pursued a degree in secondary education with specialization in biology. He graduated from Central Florida University in 1970 and began teaching in the Orlando school system. Returning to his home state in 1972, he took up residence in Yuma where he worked for the U.S. Geological Survey, the International Boundary and Water Commission and the public schools.

STAFF SERGEANT
ERNEST T. ALVAREZ

Hometown Unknown[1]

Army Air Corps
Gunner on B-17G
322nd Bomb Squadron, 91st Bomb Group
European Theater, 8th Air Force

Sgt. Alvarez, a ball turret gunner, was listed as missing in action on November 2, 1944. He had flown 27 missions when his Flying Fortress failed to return to Bassingbourn, England.[2]

---

1. Sgt Alvarez's name was obtained from "The Honor List Of Dead And Missing For The State Of Arizona". Names are listed by County or State At Large if county is unkown.
2. Missing Aircrew Report #10142, National Archives, Suitland, Maryland.

STAFF SERGEANT DAVID S. AVILA

PHOENIX

Army Air Corps
Entered service in August 1942
Gunner on B-24 "Lady from Bristol"
714th Bomb Squadron, 448th Bomb Group
European Theater, 8th Air Force
Air Medal with OLC

After completing his training at Lowry Field, Colorado, and Tyndall Field, Florida, David was sent to England where he was assigned to the 448th Bomb Group in Seething, Norfolk County (NE of London). From there, he began flying combat missions as a tail gunner over continental Europe in the spring of 1944.[1]

One mission he especially remembers was when his plane was forced to leave the main formation and, being a straggler, immediately attracted a swarm of German fighters. For the next several minutes the crew was in a desperate fight for their lives. With all the Liberators guns blazing away, and skillful flying by the pilots, they were able to ward off their pursuers long enough to be rescued by their own fighters. Upon landing at their base, they counted so many holes, that the "Lady" looked like a piece of Swiss cheese. His own turret bubble had taken four hits.

Discharged from the service in September 1945, David returned to his home state and worked for laundry and dry cleaning businesses in Phoenix and Glendale. In 1962 he joined his brother working at a laundry in Sunnyvale, California, and two years later opened his own business, Custom Cleaners, in Milpitas, California. This business failed but he was undaunted, and later reopened at a new location in south San Jose. This location was very successful and he went on to open two more Custom Cleaners before retiring in 1987, after his wife Josephine passed away. Mr. Avila resides in Phoenix. He has seven children, eighteen grandchildren and twenty-five great-grandchildren.

---

1. Photo courtesy of David S. Avila

LIEUTENANT APOLONIO (HAP) BARRAZA

TOLLESON

Army Air Corps
Entered Service in November 1942
Navigator on B-17G "Blythe Spirit"
711th Bomb Squadron, 447th Bomb Group
European Theater, 8th Air Force
Air Medal with 5 OLC

Hap is a graduate of Tolleson Union High School class of 1940. In June of 1944, he completed navigation training at Pan American Airways, University of Miami, Coral Gables, Florida. In the fall of 1944, after completing combat crew training in Rapid City, South Dakota, he was sent overseas to England. Assigned to the 447th Bomb Group stationed at Rattlesden about sixty miles NW of London, Hap began flying combat missions to strategic targets on the European continent.

Hap's first mission was the one he remembers most.

> *The target was located in one of the most heavily defended areas in all of Germany—the Leipzig area—where synthetic oil production was centered. On the bomb run to the target, the lead aircraft in our group of 36 B-17s was shot down, along with four others, and there was a mad scramble to avoid hitting parts of the disintegrating aircraft. We*

ended up flying alone with no idea where the rest of the planes were, and we headed back to England on our own. Soon, a B-17 tacked on off our right wing and then another off to our left wing. Before we knew what was happening, we were leading a whole group (not ours). They too had lost their leader and were just trying to get back to England as best as they could. Here we were, on our first mission and flying lead for an entire group from the First Air Division. Eventually, we located our own group in the Third Air Division and returned to base. On this same mission, one of the navigators in our squadron posthumously received the Medal of Honor. His aircraft was hit by flak and he was wounded by a piece of shrapnel. He refused a shot of morphine until he had guided his pilot to within sight of the English coastline. Lt. Femoyer died as his aircraft was landing. His locker was near mine and I saw his bloodied equipment bag (A-3) in front of his locker where his crew's bombardier was sorting things out.

Hap and members of his combat crew, November 1944.[1] Back Row L to R: Al Bartlett, Shel Siegel, Linn Hodge, and H. Barraza. Front Row L to R: Ken Cooper, Walt Manaker, Will Schirmer, Lyle Frye, Howie Robertson.

After completing his combat tour of thirty-five missions, Hap returned to the US and was stationed at Ellington Field, Texas, when the war ended.

Upon separation from the service in October 1945, he returned to Arizona and farmed in the Phoenix area. He attended Arizona State College (now Arizona State University) from 1948 to 1951. During the Korean War he was recalled to extended active duty and remained in the Air Force as a career officer. In 1958, while stationed at Eglin AFB, Florida, he obtained a B.S. Degree in Management from Florida State University. He held ratings as a Master Navigator and Electronics Warfare Officer and finished his military career as a Staff Intelligence

---

1. Photo courtesy of Hap Barraza.

Officer with the North American Air Defense Command (NORAD). Hap retired from the Air force in March 1969 with the rank of major. His decorations include the Air Medal with 5 OLC, WWII Victory Medal, European, African, Middle Eastern Combat Medal with 2 battle stars, Army Commendation Medal, National Defense Service Medal with 1 battle star, AFLSA with 5 OLC, Air Force Reserve Medal, Air Force Outstanding Unit Award, Good Conduct Medal, Joint Service Commendation Medal, and Small Arms Expert Marksman Ribbon.

Since returning to Phoenix, Hap has been self-employed in bookkeeping and income tax services. He is married to the former Cleta Maxine Sessums. They have three children, three grandchildren, and two great-grandchildren.

STAFF SERGEANT FERNANDO (FRITZ) BELIS

TUCSON

Army Air Corps
Gunner on A-20G-35 Bomber
645th Bomb Squadron, 410th Bomb Group
European Theater, 9th Air Force
Air Medal with 3 OLC

On July 25, 1944 Sergeant Belis was killed in action when his plane was hit by enemy flak on a bombing mission to St. Gilles, France, and crashed near St. Lo. The pilot 1st Lt. George A. Johnson of Neptune City, New Jersey, was the only survivor of the three-man crew. The other flyer killed was turret gunner Armando S. Jacques of Los Angeles, California.[1] Sergeant Belis was twenty-two years old.

---

1. Missing Aircrew Report #9053, National Archives, Suitland, Maryland.

TECHNICAL SERGEANT RAYMOND BERNAL

TUCSON

Army Air Corps
Entered Service in September 1942
Flight Engineer/Gunner on B-24 "Solid John"
515th Bomb Squadron, 376th Bomb Group
Mediterranean Theater, 9th, 12th &15th Air Force
Air Medal with 7 OLC

Graduating from Tucson High School in the class of 1942, Raymond entered the Army Air Corps that same year. He trained at various army airfields located in Texas, Kansas, Florida, and Iceland before being sent overseas to the Mediterranean Theater. From air bases in Benghazi, Libya; Cairo, Egypt; Tunis, Tunisia; Sicily, and Italy, he completed fifty-two combat missions against Axis targets. His most unforgettable mission was the bombing of the Ploesti oil fields and refineries. Ploesti, located in eastern Rumania was a major source of petroleum for the Axis and therefore heavily guarded with fighter aircraft and anti-aircraft gun batteries. To avoid detection, the squadrons of B-24 Liberators approached their targets at low altitude, but it was to no avail. Damage to the Axis was substantial, but the Americans also suffered heavy losses. Out of 178 B-24s that took off from North Africa on the August, 1943 mission, only 33 ever flew again.[1]

---

1. The American Heritage Picture History of WWII by C.L. Sulzberger.

After the war Raymond worked for the US department of Agriculture in Mexico for six years. Returning to Tucson, he was employed by Lucky's supermarket stores until his retirement in the mid 1980s.

STAFF SERGEANT AMADO BERRELLEZ

NOGALES

Army Air Corps
Entered Service in June 1942
Gunner on B-17 "El Diablo"
346th Bomb Squadron, 99th Bomb Group
Mediterranean Theater, 12th Air Force
Air Medal with 12 OLC

Upon receiving his gunner's wings at Harlingen Field, Texas in August of 1942, Amado was assigned to combat crew training in Boise, Idaho. In early 1943, he was sent to North Africa where he began flying missions with the "Fighting Ninety-Ninth". Most missions were to bomb enemy aerodromes (airfields) and railroad marshalling yards on the Italian peninsula. The first of Amado's fifty missions was to Villacidro Aerodrome on March 31, 1943 and the final was to Pomigliano Aerodrome five months later on September 6th. One major air battle he participated in occurred on July 5, 1943, when twenty-seven B-17s bombed Gerbini Aerodrome on the island of Sicily. An estimated one-hundred enemy fighters, consisting of Me-109s, FW190s, and Macchi 202s, intercepted the bombers before, during, and after the bombing run. Enemy losses amounted to thirty-eight fighters destroyed in the air, eleven fighters probably destroyed, and one fighter damaged, against the loss of three B-17s. The mission was a complete success with the destruction of twenty aircraft on the ground and severe damage to many installations including hangars, fuel supplies and ammunition dumps. This single mission provided a major blow to enemy defenses in time for the Allied invasion of Sicily five days later.[1]

After completing his combat tour, Sgt Berrellez returned to Arizona for his new assignment as a gunner instructor at Davis Monthan Field near Tucson. He remained there until his discharge from the service in 1945.

From October 1950 to October 1951, Amado was activated for duty in Korea where he served as a gunner on B-29s and B-36s. During the 1950s and until 1965, he was employed for the US Navy in Litchfield Park, Arizona, as an aircraft electrician. He then transferred to North Island Naval Air Station in San Diego, California where he became a quality assurance specialist until his retirement in August 1983.

---

1. Fifteenth Air Force document dated June 7, 1944 that describes accomplishments of the 99th Bomb Group for unit citation. (12th AF became 15th AF when unit moved to Italy). Document courtesy of Amado Berrellez.

STAFF SERGEANT INOCENTE (CHENTE) R. BOLTAREZ

HAYDEN

Army Air Corps
Entered Service 1943
Gunner on A-20 Havoc Bomber
387th Bomb Squadron, 312th Bomb Group
Pacific Theater, 5th Air Force

Sergeant Boltarez was a graduate of Hayden High School class of 1940. He was reported missing in action in the Southwest Pacific on March 15th, 1944 when his A-20 bomber failed to return from a mission to New Guinea. Eyewitness accounts indicated the plane in which he was a crewmember was hit by enemy anti-aircraft fire at the target. A parachute was seen to leave the disabled bomber approximately four miles west of Kairuri Island. Subsequent searches failed to find the missing aircraft or any of its crew.[1]

---

1. Letter to Sgt. Boltarez's mother, Mrs. Carmen R. Boltarez, from Headquarters, Army Air Forces dated July 25, 1944. Courtesy of Carmen Boltarez (Sgt Boltarez's sister-in-law).

```
11  FN  Q 33 Govt

              WMU  WASHINGTON DC 355PM April 1 1944

MRS CARMEN R BOLTAREZ
       P.O. BOX 1004
              HAYDEN Ariz.

THE SECRETARY OF WAR DESIRES  ME TO EXPRESS HIS DEEP REGRET
THAT YOUR SON STAFF SERGEANT  INOCENTE R BOLTAREZ HAS BEEN
REPORTED MISSING IN ACTION SINCE  FIFTEEN MARCH OVER  BAGUINA PERIOD
LETTER FOLLOWS
              DUNLOP
                ACTING THE ADJUTANT GENERAL
                              310pm
```

Sgt. Boltarez's mother, Carmen, received this telegram two weeks after he was reported missing.[2]

---

2. Copy of telegram courtesy of Carmen Boltarez.

STAFF SERGEANT INOCENTE (CHENTE) R. BOLTAREZ

Chente Boltarez (far left) and friends at the Biltmore Bowl, of the Biltmore Hotel, in Los Angeles on April 3, 1943. This was during his training period before going overseas. Others in photo are L to R: Arnold L. Salazar, Dave L. Bowman and Jerry J. Beitacchi.[3]

---

3. Photo courtesy of Mrs. Carmen Boltarez.

STAFF SERGEANT EPIFANIO (EPPY) P. CAMPOS

SAFFORD

Army Air Corps
Entered Service in June 1942
Flight Engineer/Gunner on B-17
423rd Bomb Squadron, 306th Bomb Group
European Theater, 8th Air Force
Distinguished Flying Cross, Purple Heart,
Air Medal with 6 OLC

After graduating from Safford High School in the class of 1940, Eppy was employed at the Del Monte Food market in Safford prior to entering the service. By December 1942 his training to become a flight engineer and gunner had taken him to Sheppard Field in Texas, and McDill Field in Florida. Other training fields were Boise Field in Idaho, Wendover Field in Utah and Victorville Field in California. The types of aircraft he trained on were B-26 medium and B-17 heavy bombers.

Stationed in Bedford England with the "Mighty Eighth" during 1944, Eppy completed 35 bombing missions to targets in Germany. Some of the more perilous flights were to the heavily air-defended areas around Frankfurt, Leipzig, Saarbrucken, Berlin, Lechfeld, Oberpfaffenhofen and Liege. It was over Liege on May 31, 1944 that he was wounded in the neck by flak shrapnel. Recuperating for a week, he did not fly again until D-day June 6, when his squadron bombed the beaches of Normandy just 30 seconds before Allied forces stormed ashore.

Returning to the States in August 1945, he was stationed at Victorville where he trained new crew chiefs until his discharge in October 1945. He returned to Safford and began attending Gila Junior College, majoring in Accounting. Since 1947, Eppy has lived in Southern California where he operates his own landscaping and gardening business.

TECHNICAL SERGEANT SERVANDO B. CARRILLO

SUPERIOR

Army Air Corps
Entered Service in December 1942
Radio Operator/Gunner on B-17 and B-24 "Libra"
834th Bomb Squadron, 486th Bomb Group
European Theater, 8th Air Force
China-Burma-India Theater, 10th Air Force
Distinguished Flying Cross, Air Medal with 4 OLC

Graduating from Superior High School in the Class of 1942, Servando spent most of 1943 learning the skills of a radio operator/gunner. He trained at Scott Field in Illinois in the basics of radio operation and later at Davis-Monthan in Arizona on B-17 and B-24 bombers. Sent overseas to England, the nineteen-year-old sergeant began flying combat missions to strategic targets in Germany. "Every mission was unique unto itself," he states. However, because of their intensity, the missions he remembers most were to targets in Hamburg, Berlin, Bremen, and the Ruhr Valley. On June 6, 1944, he participated in the "D-Day" invasion of France. After completing his tour with the 8th Air Force, he began a second tour with the 10th AF in the China-Burma-India Theater. There he flew over the Himalayas ("Flying the Hump") in operations against the Japanese.

With the war over and the help from the GI Bill, Servando enrolled at Arizona State Teachers College (now Arizona State University). He obtained his Bachelor of Arts Degree in 1950 and Masters of Arts in 1960. He was a teacher and coach in Superior schools before becoming Principal of the Elementary School and later became Superintendent of the Superior Unified School District. Servando married Maria Arvizu of Florence, Arizona in 1951. They have eight children.[1]

---

1. Photo courtesy of Servando B. Carrillo.

LIEUTENANT
IGNACIO (NASH) CASTRO

NOGALES

US Navy
Entered Service in November 1942
Pilot on PBY5A
VPB 54 Squadron
Pacific Theater
Air Medal

A graduate of Nogales High class of 1937, Nash was employed by the National Park Service at Grand Canyon National Park before entering the Navy as an aviation cadet in the fall of 1942. Basic flight training at Lynchburg College, Virginia and Bunker Hill Naval Air Station, Indiana was completed in June 1943. It was at Lynchburg that he learned to fly Piper Cubs and at Bunker Hill NAS that he checked out in Stearmans prior to being sent to Pensacola, Florida for advanced training on SNV, SNJ, and SNB type aircraft. In November of

1943 he received his gold pilot wings and a commission in the Naval Reserve. Ensign Castro then proceeded to Jacksonville NAS in Florida where he honed his flying skills on SNBs and PBY patrol planes. Assigned to the Pacific Theater, he flew patrol, bombing, and rescue missions from bases throughout the South Pacific. During the thirteen-month period he was overseas, he completed over 200 missions from posts at Midway Island, Funafuti, Guadalcanal, New Hebrides, Admiralty Islands, New Guinea, Palau Islands, and the Philippines. He participated in such major operations as the Palau Islands and Philippines in particular.

Returning to the States in April 1945, Nash was training in other naval aircraft at Jacksonville NAS and Alameda NAS until discharged from the service in December 1945.[1]

Nash resumed his career with the National Park Service upon his return to civilian life. During the next 23 years with the Park Service he held various administrative positions in Hawaii, Nebraska, and the last position being the Director of the National Capital Parks in Washington, D.C. From September 1969 until retirement in April 1990, he was Executive Director of Palisades Interstate Park Commission in New York-New Jersey. He maintains a practice as a consultant on Natural and Historic Resources Management. He is the author of "The Land of Pele", and various articles and publications. In 1966, he was presented the Department of Interior's highest honor, the Distinguished Service Award. In 1970 and 1979, he was recipient of the American Scenic and Historic Preservation Society's Pugsley Medals. In 1990, he received the Horace Marden Albright Scenic Preservation Medal. He has served trusteeships, directorships, and other executive level and advisory positions for more than thirty organizations. Some of these include Executive Director, Director and President of the White House Historical Association; Executive Secretary of the Committee for the Preservation of The White House; Chairman of the committee that built the memorial to President Johnson; Founding

---

1. Photo courtesy of Grace Castro.

President of the National Wildflower Research Center (now the Lady Bird Johnson Wildflower Center in Texas); White House liason for the National Park Service, 1961-68; served as trustee or director of several Rockefeller Family boards, including Jackson Hole Preserve, Inc., the American Conservation Association, the Woodstock Foundation, Inc. and Historic Hudson Valley.

Nash holds honorary doctorates from St. Thomas Aquinas College, Sparkill, N.Y., and Mount St. Mary's College, Newburgh, N.Y. He attended George Washington University in Washington, D.C.

Nash is married to the former Bette Woolsey, of Tucson. They have two children and seven grandchildren.

STAFF SERGEANT VICTOR V. CERVANTEZ

MORENCI

Army Air Corps
Entered Service in December 1941
Gunner on B-24
409th Bomb Squadron, 93rd Bomb Group
European Theater, 8th Air Force
Distinguished Flying Cross, Air Medal with 3 OLC

Victor was 18 years old when he enlisted in the Army Air Corps on December 1, 1941. Just six days later, the US entered the Second World War when the Japanese attacked Pearl Harbor. During the great mobilization period of 1942 and 1943, Victor was stationed for training and general duty at numerous bases throughout the continental US, beginning with basic training in Biloxi, Mississippi. He later spent time at Hammer Field in Fresno, California, Lowery Field Colorado, Las Vegas, Nevada and finally pre-combat crew training as a nose turret-gunner on B-24s at Alamogordo, New Mexico, in late 1943.

Arriving in England in January of 1944, Victor was sent to Hardwick in the county of Norfolk (NE of London) for duty with the 8th AF. On May 22 he began flying bombing missions to enemy targets in Germany and France. Many of his thirty missions were in support of the air offensive just prior to, during, and after the June 6th D-Day invasion of Europe by Allied forces.

After the war and until his death in 1964 at age 41, Victor was employed at the Phelps Dodge mining operations in Morenci. He was married to the former Anita Pedregon of Clifton. They had four children.

TECH SERGEANT FRANCISCO J. COLUNGA

NOGALES

Army Air Corps
Entered Service November 1942
Radio Operator/Gunner on B-24J
320th Bomb Squadron, 90th Bomb Group
Pacific Theater, 5th Air Force
Air Medal

On September 3, 1944 while on a mission to Langoan Airdrome on Celebes Island in Indonesia, Sgt. Colunga was killed when his B-24 Liberator was intercepted by enemy fighters immediately after the bombing run. Two crewmembers were reported to have bailed out. The plane crashed approximately two miles west of the target.[1] Sgt. Colunga had been overseas in the Pacific since March 1944. He was a graduate of Nogales High School class of 1940.

---

1. Missing Aircrew Report #9017, National Archives, Suitland, Maryland.

SERGEANT GUSTAVO E. CONTRERAS

TUCSON

Army Air Corps
Gunner on B-17
532nd Squadron, 381st Bomb Group
European Theater, 8th Air Force

On November 26, 1944 while on his 8th mission, Sergeant Contreras's plane was shot down by enemy aircraft near Apeldoorn Holland. His plane was returning to base at Ridgewell, England from a bombing mission to Altenbecken, Germany. Eyewitness accounts stated that Gus bailed out but was killed by heavy ground fire while descending to the ground.[1] Gus had just turned 20 years old on November 15th.[2]

---

1. Missing Aircrew Report #11205, National Archives, Suitland, Maryland.
2. John Comer the author of Combat Crew writes about his own combat experiences while stationed with the 381st Bomb Group at Ridgewell from July to December 1943.

CAPTAIN
LUIS BONILLAS COPPOLA

TUCSON/NOGALES

Army Air Corps
Entered Service in August 1942
Pilot on B-17
526th Bomb Squadron, 379th Bomb Group
European Theater, 8th Air Force
Air Medal with 6 OLC

Born in Arizona of an Italian father and Mexican mother, Luis spent his childhood growing up on both sides of the Arizona/Sonora border. After graduating from Tucson High School in the class of 1938, he enrolled at the University of Arizona as an engineering student. He was in his third year at the U of A when the United States entered the Second World War. Little did he know that this event would forever change his career plans to become a mining engineer.

In the fall of 1942, Luis was accepted as a cadet in the Army Air Corps and began a yearlong period of pilot training. First he went to San Antonio, Texas for preflight school. This was followed by primary pilot training on Fairchild PT-19s at Muskogee, Oklahoma, and basic pilot training on Vultee BT-13s at Coffeyville, Kansas. The final phase was advanced training on AT-6s at Victoria, Texas, and it was there in October of 1943 that he was awarded his silver pilot wings and gold bars of a second lieutenant. He was then selected to attend the basic instructor course at Randolph Field, Texas, where, upon completion, he became a flying instructor at Coffeeville.

In December of 1944, after having completed pre-combat training on B-17s, Luis left the USA for overseas duty with the 8th Air Force. He was assigned to the 526th Bomb Squadron of the 379th Bomb Group stationed at Kimbolton, Huntingdonshire, England. From this base located about 45 miles north of London, he began flying missions in January 1945 to strategic targets in Germany. Three months and thirty-five missions later he completed his combat tour. Shortly after this, the war in Europe ended and the recently promoted Captain returned to the USA and civilian life.

In 1949, Luis, along with a partner, began operating an airline in Baja California. Flying a war surplus C-47, he carried mail, passengers and cargo between the Baja peninsula and the Mexican mainland. Diversifying, he entered the hotel business in 1952 with the purchase of the Los Arcos Hotel La Paz. He later opened other hotel properties such as the Gran Baja La Paz and Hotel Finisterra in Cabo San Lucas on Baja's southern tip. These successful ventures were mentioned in the December 1989 issue of National Geographic magazine that featured an article about Baja California.

Luis and members of his combat crew.[1] Back Row L to R: Stanley Fritz, Fred Farrel, David Kaufman, Luis, Bill Elsdorn, Jerry Hill. Front Row L to R: Bob Hardorn, Ed Weinz, Harry Motsinger, Mike Torre

---

1. Photo courtesy of Luis B. Coppola.

LIEUTENANT VALDEMAR A. CORDOVA

PHOENIX

Army Air Corps
Entered Service in August 1940
Pilot on B-17 "Virgin Sturgeon"
570th Squadron, 390th Bomb Group
European Theater, 8th Air Force
Distinguished Flying Cross, Air Medal with 3 OLC, Purple Heart

---

The following article appeared in the Arizona Republic on September 13, 1943.

Experiences As Fortress Pilot Told By Phoenician

The U. S. Army Air Forces builds rough little 20-by-20-foot shacks in the center of the 500-foot targets used for Flying Fortress bombing practice.

Such a shack, said Second Lt. Valdemar Cordova of Phoenix, co-pilot and fire control officer of a Fort, "looks like a pinhead from 30,000 feet."

Yet the bombardier in Cordova's Fort, Lt. Edward Morgan of Chicago, made the almost unbelievable record of "hitting the shack" three times in succession, all during one day and one training mission.

Efficiency Shown

Lieutenant Cordova told the story as a means of emphasizing the hair-like precision which is enabling American bomber crews to blast wide the productive facilities, communications systems and other vital targets of the axis home and battle fronts.

Member of a pioneer Arizona family, a native of Phoenix, the young flier is the son of Louis Cordova, foreman at the Aluminum Company of America plant, and Mrs. Cordova. He was a basketball star in Phoenix Union High School prior to his joining the service three years ago. Today, at 21, he is one of the key officers aboard a plane which represents in equipment alone an investment of more than $250,000.

Target Described

"How big does the 500-foot target circle look from 30,000 feet?" Lieutenant Cordova was asked.

The flier curled the index finger of his right hand to press against the thumb and indicated an insignificant circle.

The four officers and six enlisted men who serve aboard his Fort came from all sections of the country. To guarantee that the group will make a happy and smooth-working team, the crew gets 50 hours of special shake-down training so that if animosities develop, shifts of men can be made until the 10 men do shape up as a team, Lieutenant Cordova said.

The pilot and co-pilot, the bombardier, the navigator, the aerial gunners all have come from their separate schools and training backgrounds working as individuals until they come to their assignment to one Fort. They become a close-knit and clannish organization in no time.

Never Misses

"I have never seen our bombardier miss the target yet," Lieutenant Cordova said, as proudly as if he were the bombardier himself.

Lieutenant Cordova is clean and slim and straight as a fine knife, as delicately balanced, and with as keen an edge. He came to his commission the hard way, after service in the ranks.

His first service, after joining the army in August, 1940, was as a private in the medical corps at Fort Bliss. He transferred to the cavalry, then obtained a specialist's rating in personnel work. Transferring to the air forces, he rose to the rank of staff sergeant before taking and passing his his cadet examination in March, 1942.

He received his primary flight training at Cuero, Tex., his basic at Waco, Tex. It was at Waco, also, where he obtained his wings after going through twin-engine pilot school.

Landing Is Vivid

He remembers particularly vividly one landing with a B-17 during training, with a full 10-man crew aboard. It was at a state of Washington airport.

"Two of my engines were on fire and billowing smoke as I headed for the field," he said. "Then one of the other engines started smoking. I notified the control tower I would have to make an emergency landing.

"With two engines out and a third engine smoking it was no use to leave on the fourth, so I cut the remaining motor and came in without power. We landed all right. But I certainly sweated for a while."

Lieutenant Cordova's Fort has not yet been in overseas service. He has two brothers in service, Seaman Second Class Alex Cordova, in coast guard radio school at Atlantic City, N. J., and Sgt. Gilbert Cordova of the Army Air Forces, San Bernardino, Calif.

Here on leave, Lieutenant Cordova will return to his training shortly.

After completing his training in late 1943, Val boarded the Queen Elizabeth for England. Stationed with the 8th Air Force at Edge of Ipswitch, Pahrham Airdrome (about 60 miles from London), he began flying combat missions to targets in Germany. On January 29, 1944 while on his 15th mission, his B-17 was shot down by enemy fire over Frankfurt. Bailing out with the rest of his crew, Val was captured and interned at Stalag Luft 1 until the war ended one and a half years later.

Val and members of his combat crew in April 1943 prior to going overseas to England.[1] Front Row L to R: Craven, Ovadal, Ross, Lobue, Plouff. Back Row L to R: Jacobsen, Morgan, Cordova, Harding. Crewmember Fritz is absent from photo.

Returning to civilian life, Val took advantage of the educational opportunities offered to veterans though the GI Bill. He graduated from Arizona State College (now Arizona State University) and later from the University of Arizona with a law degree. He practiced law in Phoenix until June of 1965 when he became a Maricopa County Superior Court Judge. After being recommended by Senator Dennis Deconcini, Val was appointed in July 1979 as a Federal District Court Judge. He remained on the Federal bench in Phoenix until an extended illness forced him to step down. Judge Cordova passed away on June 18, 1988.

---

1. Photo courtesy of Gloria Cordova.

TECHNICAL SERGEANT GILBERT S. CORONA

YUMA

Army Air Corps
Entered Service June 1942
Radio Operator/Gunner on B-26 "Frances John" and "Dorothy Ann"
441st Bomb Squadron, 320th Bomb Group
Mediterranean Theater, 12th Air Force
Air Metal with 2 OLC

Gilbert is a 1940 graduate of Yuma Union High School. He had completed two years at Northern Arizona State Teachers College (now Northern Arizona University) when he entered the service. After training at airfields in Fort Meyers and Avon Park, Florida, he was sent overseas to North Africa. From Dijeda, south of Tunis, he began flying missions in support of the Allied invasion at Salerno in southern Italy. He also flew missions to the islands of Sicily and Sardinia before his unit was moved to Sardinia. From here he flew missions to southern France and to targets on the Italian Peninsula at Monte Casino and in support of the impending Anzio Invasion. On January 21, 1944, while on his 25th mission, his B-26 Marauder the "Frances John" was hit several times by heavy flak and caught fire. Gilbert and one other parachuted out, but five crewmembers went down with the plane near Orvietto north of Rome. This mission to bomb Decimo and bridges over the Tiber River resulted in heavy plane losses to his squadron.

Along with other airmen who had suffered the same fate, Gilbert was captured and taken by freight train to Stalag Luft III, Sagan, southeast of Berlin. Later, when the Russians advanced from the east through Poland, the POWs were moved south by marching and rail to Nuremberg. Because of heavy Allied bombardment of this city, they were again marched south, finally reaching Moorsburg outside of Munich. It was there in April 1945 that Gilbert was liberated by General Patton's troops. Gilbert spent 16 months as a prisoner, and recommends the books *Kriege* by Kenneth W. Simmons and A *Wartime Log* by Art and Lee Beltrone, which describes life in the POW camps.

Returning to civilian life, Gilbert completed his college education in 1947 at Northern Arizona State Teachers College. For the next thirty-seven years, he taught at Seligman and Flagstaff high schools. He also coached football and baseball and was very active in the Arizona Coaches Association, serving as president in 1968. He has been inducted into the Arizona Coaches Hall of Fame.

Mr. Corona is married to the former Grace Kenoski of Canonsburg, Pennsylvania. They have two children and three grandchildren.

FIRST LIEUTENANT
VIDAL J. CORTEZ

MESA

Army Air Corps
Entered Service November 1941
Pilot on B-24 "Little Jo Toddy"
23rd Bomb Squadron, 5th Bomb Group
Pacific Theater, 13th Air Force
Air Medal with 8 OLC

Vidal is a graduate of Mesa High School class of 1940. He entered the service just prior to the Japanese attack on Pearl Harbor. While stationed at Lowry Army Airfield, Denver, Colorado in early 1942, he and several of his GI buddies decided to take the aviation cadet exams being conducted. He was the only one of his group who passed the tests.[1] Accepted for pilot training, he was sent to Maxwell Field, Montgomery, Alabama for preflight school. His primary flight school was at Camden, South Carolina where he trained on the Stearman PT-17 and soloed after completing approximately ten hours of hands-on instruction. For the next phase, basic flight school, he was sent to Cochran Field in Macon, Georgia for training on the Vultee BT-13.

His advanced flight school was completed at Turner Field in Albany, Georgia, where he trained on the Curtiss AT-9, Beechcraft AT-10 and the North American AT-6. There he received his pilot wings and officer's commission in April 1943. Lieutenant Cortez was then assigned to Biggs Field, El Paso, Texas for crew training on the B-24 Liberator, the heavy bomber he would be flying in combat. After picking up a new B-24 in Lincoln, Nebraska, he and his crew departed from Fairfield Suisun in California for the South Pacific in August of 1943. Assigned to the 5th Bomb Group with the 13th Air Force at Esperitu Santo in the New Hebrides (now Vanuatu), Vidal and his crew began flying bombing missions against Japanese installations. During the next six months, as 1st officer of the "Little Jo Toddy," he flew forty-five combat missions from Esperito Santo, Guadalcanal and Bougainville in support of the advancing Allied forces throughout the Pacific Theater.

Returning to the US in late 1944, Lt. Cortez was assigned to the Air Training Command. During this period, he served as a B-25 instructor at Enid Field, Enid, Alabama, and instrument flying instructor at Randolph Field, San Antonio, Texas. He was also a flight instructor at Dothan, Alabama, where he trained Latin American cadets from Mexico and South America. When the war ended in the late summer of 1945, Vidal remained in the service and was stationed at Turner Field, Albany, Georgia. In October 1946 he was assigned to Guatemala City with the Air Mission as an instrument flying instructor to Guatemalan Air Force pilots.

During his tour of duty as an instructor he trained many student pilots from various countries including China, France, Guatemala and Mexico. He was awarded honorary pilot wings from each of these

---

1. Photo courtesy of Vidal J. Cortez

countries. In another assignment he worked at the Adjutant General's office in New York City where he assisted in compiling an English/Spanish dictionary of aircraft terms. While maintaining his flight status at Mitchell Field on Long Island he also logged many hours commuting on the New York subway system.

In January 1950 he was discharged from extended active duty and was assigned to the Ready Reserve on flying status. Moving to the West Coast in 1950, he continued his education by enrolling at Mount Vernon Junior college in Mt. Vernon, Washington. From here he matriculated to Western Washington University in Bellingham, Washington, where he obtained a BA degree in economics and pre-law in 1955.

Returning to his home state in 1956, Vidal held various civil service positions at Williams Air Force Base. In 1970 he retired from active reserve status with the rank of lieutenant colonel. In 1986 he retired from his position as the Base Budget Director at Williams AFB. His decorations include the Air Medal with eight OLC, American Theater of War Medal, WWII Victory Medal, National Defense Service Medal, and American Campaign Medal.

Vidal is married to the former Gladys Meyer of Mt. Vernon, Washington. They have three children and three grandchildren.

LIEUTENANT HECTOR E. DEVARGAS

MORENCI

Army Air Corps
Entered Service in 1942
Bombardier on B-17F
524th Squadron, 379th Bomb Group
European Theater, 8th Air Force
Air Medal with 2 OLC

A graduate of Morenci High class of 1939, Hector is the younger brother of Roger Vargas (see page 217). Hector had his name changed and is listed on military records as DeVargas. From 1940 to 1942 Hector was a member of the Arizona National Guard. Accepted as a cadet for training in the Army Air Corps, he received his bombardier wings and commission at Roswell, New Mexico in early 1943. After completing pre-combat training, he was assigned to the 379th heavy bombardment group with the 8th Air Force, stationed in Kimbolton, England (about 45 miles N of London). He began flying combat missions to targets in Germany in July, 1943. On August 17, 1943 he wrote the following letter to his father, Pasqual Vargas, after returning from the 8th Air Force's first mission to bomb Schweinfurt in Germany.[1]

England—E.T.O.
August 17, 1943

Hello Dad,

I have never been so tired before. My hands are still jittery with the shock of the guns. I may be able to get a good sleep tonight. Our raid today will be old headlines when you receive this, but we gave Jerry hell. It is rugged, dad. Roger had a chance in the Pacific. We do not go out in single plane raids. We talk in terms of hundreds, and more.

There is much that I wish I could tell you. I am exhausted and must get some sleep. I do not know how much longer it will go on. It is a matter of luck. The newspapers do not tell the truth. My god, dad, if the people over there could only realize what is happening over here. People are out to exterminate each other. The English do not want Italy to quit the war. They want to bomb Italy out of existence. These people have suffered much and only wish for revenge. Such is the world and the inhabitants in it. They are right in feeling as they do, but how will it end? I do not have much time now. Write as often as you can. Perhaps I will hear from you. I am tired and may have to go again tomorrow. How is everybody? I wonder how little Diane is doing.

Hector

On October 14, 1943, while participating on the "Second Schweinfurt" mission, Hector was killed when his Flying Fortress, under attack, crashed head-on with a German Me-109.[2] This mission is infa-

---

1. Letter and photos courtesy of Roger Vargas
2. Missing Aircrew Report #1353, National Archives, Suitland, Maryland.

mous in the history of the Air Corps during WWII because over sixty B-17s were shot down going into and returning from the target. It is called "Second Schweinfurt" to distinguish it from the first mission to Schweinfurt which occurred on August 17, 1943, also with heavy losses. Schweinfurt, a city in Bavaria, was where many of Germany's ball-bearing factories were located and was, as a result, heavily defended by fighter aircraft and anti-aircraft batteries.

At this stage of the air war in Europe, fighter escort coverage for bombers all the way to Schweinfurt and back was not yet available. The P-51 D model was still under development and would not be operational for combat until early 1944. With its faster Rolls Royce designed engine and long range capability, the P-51 D Mustang would improve the chances of bomber crews completing the fabled 25 missions. Unfortunately, for Hector and his fellow crewmembers, this superior aircraft arrived four months too late.

Hector is buried at the Lorraine American cemetery, St. Avold, France.

Lt.Devargas and his combat crew in 1943. Back Row L to R: S. Garfield, T. Carlson, E. Growman, H. Devargas, E. Grossman. Front Row L to R: F. Landis, W.Forsythe, J. Earenzeller, A. Skelton, R.Gray.

FLIGHT OFFICER BENJAMIN DIAZ

PHOENIX

Army Air Corps
Entered Service in February 1944
Flight Engineer on B-29
444th Heavy Bombardment Group

Aviation Cadet Ben Diaz began preflight training in early 1944 at Washington State College where he took courses in English, math and military history. He was then sent to the San Antonio Cadet Center in Texas, where in January 1945 he completed Flight Engineer training. Next he proceeded to Hando Air Field near San Antonio and Smoky Hill Air Field near Salina, Kansas for B-29 combat crew familiarization.[1] Prior to being assigned to a squadron overseas, the war ended with the Japanese surrender on

1. Photo courtesy of Benjamin Diaz

September 2, 1945. Discharged from the service in February 1946, he returned to Phoenix. In 1947 Ben began civil service employment as an avionics technician at Litchfield Park Navy Facility. When this facility closed in 1966, he joined the US Air Force Reserve at Luke Air Force Base where he remained until his retirement in 1985.

STAFF SERGEANT
JULIO R. DIAZ

PHOENIX

Army Air Corps
Entered Service in February 1943
Gunner on B-24 "Bathless"
392nd Bomb Squadron, 30th Bomb Group
Pacific Theater, 7th Air Force
Distinguished Flying Cross, Air Medal with 5 OLC
Navy Air Medal, Purple Heart

After training at army airfields in California, Colorado, Idaho, and Texas, Julio, age twenty, was sent to the Pacific Theater of Operations. From Kwajalein Atoll where he was based with the 7th Air Force, he flew his first mission on April 17, 1944. This mission, to bomb the Japanese island of Saipan, would be one he would never forget. It was a combined operation of army and navy units flying B-24s and its navy version, PB4Ys. Returning from the target, Julio's plane begin "escorting" a damaged navy bomber, and for the next 25 minutes, they managed to repel a swarm of enemy fighters attacking the two stragglers. As the ball turret gunner, Sgt Diaz shared credit for shooting down a Zero and credited with a probable for another. After a long flight, the navy plane was able to return to its base but the army plane was not so fortunate. Suffering heavy damage and running out of fuel, they were forced to ditch in rough seas about 280 miles short of their base. Escaping into four life rafts, the crew spent six nights and five days adrift in the Pacific. An attempt to rescue them by a navy PBY seaplane was dashed when the plane began leaking as they climbed aboard. With the army crew back in their rafts and the navy crew in their own rafts, they spent the night near the doomed PBY before being picked up the next day by a navy destroyer.[1]

Sgt. Diaz went on to complete 39 more combat missions as a ball turret gunner before returning to the States as a gunnery instructor at Yuma Air Field.

Julio with members of his combat crew. Julio is in the back row, 3rd from left.[2]

---

1. From news item in the Arizona Rebublic on May 9, 1944, titled "Phoenix Airman Takes Part In Saving Crippled Plane".
2. Photo courtesy of Julio R. Diaz.

After returning to civilian life, Julio began employment for the US Postal Service where he remained until his retirement in 1978. He also served in the Arizona National Guard and Army Reserve for twenty-four years until retiring in 1970 with the rank of First Sergeant. Mr. Diaz passed away in February 1995. His wife Conception, five children, six grandchildren and seven great-grandchildren survive him.

CAPTAIN
JOSEPH S. DOMINGUEZ

NACO

Army Air Corps
Entered Service in February 1943
Pilot on C-47 and C-54
Air Transport Command
Pacific Theater
Air Medal

Joseph graduated from Bisbee High School in the class of 1941. In February 1943, he was accepted into the Aviation Cadet program and began primary pilot training at Winfield Field, Missouri on PT-19 aircraft. After completing his basic flight training at Sikeston Field, Missouri on BT-13s, he was sent to Blackland Field in Waco, Texas for advanced flight school. In this final phase of pilot training he learned to fly twin engine Cessna UC-78 and UC-9 aircraft. In March 1944, he received his silver wings and a commission as a 2nd lieutenant. After graduation, Joseph remained at Blackland Field for six months as a flight instrument instructor. His next assignment was flying C-47 transports or "Gooney Birds" from airfields in St. Joseph, Missouri, Long Beach, and San Francisco (Hamilton Field), California before heading overseas to the Pacific Theater in early 1945. From airfields in Australia, New Guinea and the Philippines he transported troops and material, and evacuated the wounded, until several months after the war had ended.

Returning to the States, he transitioned to four-engine C-54s and continued his flight duties while stationed at Fairfield Suisun Field, (now Travis AFB) California. Upon his discharge in February 1946, Captain Dominguez had logged a total of 1900 flight hours.

Back in civilian life, Joseph entered the construction and mining business in Mexico. On August 10, 2000, he passed away in Tucson. He is survived by his wife Barbara, four children and three grand children.

SERGEANT ARTHUR R. ESTRADA

PHOENIX

Army Air Corps
Entered Service July, 1942
Radio Operator/Gunner
92nd Bomb Group
European Theater, 8th Air Force

The following news item appeared in the Phoenix Gazette on May 3, 1945.

Sgt. Estrada Dies In Action

Sgt. Arthur R. Estrada, 23-year-old native Phoenician and a radioman with the U. S. Army Air Forces, was killed in action in England on on Dec. 30, according to word received here by his parents, Mr. and Mrs. Nick Estrada, Route 9, Box 29, Phoenix.

In a letter expressing regret for the death of a heroic soldier, Maj. Gen. J. A. Ulio wrote that details of the action in which Sergeant Estrada lost his life will be sent here later. The young soldier was buried with full military honors, it was related in a letter from Method C. Billy, O. M. C., Catholic chaplain of the 92nd Bombardment Group. Interment was in the military cemetery in East Anglia, England, following a requiem mass in the station chapel.

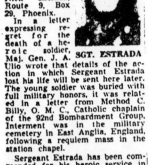

SGT. ESTRADA

Sergeant Estrada has been commended for his heroic service in citations bearing the signatures of the late President Roosevelt, Secretary of War Henry L. Stimson and Gen. H. H. Arnold, commander of the army air forces. A posthumous award of the Order of the Purple Heart for wounds received in action against the enemy has been sent here to the Phoenix soldier's parents.

General Arnold's tribute to the young soldier in a citation of honor reads: "He lived to bear his country's arms. He died to save its honor. He was a soldier, and he knew a soldier's duty. His sacrifice will help to keep aglow the flaming torch that lights our lives —that millions yet unborn may know the priceless joy of liberty. And we who pay him homage and revere his memory in solemn pride dedicate ourselves to a complete fulfillment of the task for which he so gallantly has placed his life upon the altar of man's freedom."

Sergeant Estrada entered the army on July 3, 1942, and went overseas last Nov. 2. He trained at air base training schools in Sioux Falls, S. D., Lincoln, Neb., and Yuma. He completed the course for flexible gunnery training and was graduated at the Yuma Army Air Field on July 1, 1944. He attended local schools.

His brother, Pfc. Ernest R. Estrada, with the army infantry, is in an army hospital in England. Ernest also has been awarded the Purple Heart medal for wounds received in action. Other survivors, in addition to his parents, are: five sisters, Mrs. Louise Daniels, and the Misses Virginia, Aurora, Ramona and Eloise Estrada; and a young brother, Eddie William Estrada, all of Phoenix.

CORPORAL OSCAR C. GALLEGOS

PHOENIX

Army Air Corps
Entered Service 1942
Gunner/Armorer on B-17G
331st Bomb Squadron, 94th Bomb Group
European Theater, 8th Air Force

On January 11, 1944 while on his 9th mission, waist gunner Gallegos bailed out of his crippled B-17 Flying Fortress near Lingen, Germany. Captured, he remained a prisoner until the war in Europe ended in the spring of 1945.[1]

---

1. Missing Aircrew Report #1884, National Archives, Suitland, Maryland

FIRST LIEUTENANT
EDWARD A. GARCIA

MORENCI

Army Air Corps
Entered Service in March 1942
Pilot Instructor

After graduating from Morenci High School in the class of 1936, Edward enrolled at Arizona State Teachers College (now Arizona State University). He later transferred to the University of Arizona where he graduated in 1941 with a Bachelor of Science degree in chemistry.

Entering the Army Air Corps three months after the sneak attack on Pearl Harbor, Cadet Garcia began preflight school at Kelly Field, Texas. He then went to Sikeston, Missouri for primary training where he soloed on a Fairchild PT-19. Next, he proceeded to Randolph Field, Texas where he completed basic flight school flying the BT-13. The final phase was advanced flight training in AT-6 Texans at Ellington Field, Texas. It was there he received his silver wings and commission in early 1943.

Edward and his brother Rudy, on leave in Clifton, 1944.

    Lieutenant Garcia's first assignment was to pilot Beech AT-7s at the Navigator Training School in San Marcos, Texas. While at San Marcos, he also completed the training and received the rating for navigator. His next assignment was B-24 training at Liberal, Kansas. Returning to Randolph Field in late 1944, Edward completed training on the Boeing B-29 Superfortress. This new weapon was the latest four engined, long-range bomber, which was being used exclusively in the Pacific to end the war with Japan. Among the improvements on this state-of-the-art aircraft, crewmembers no longer needed to wear heavy flight suits and oxygen masks since the ship was temperature controlled and pressurized. Edward was in B-29 pre-combat training in Lincoln, Nebraska, when he learned of the Japanese surrender.

Back in civilian life in early 1946, Edward went to work for Phelps Dodge in El Paso, Texas, before joining FMC Corporation in New Jersey, as a chemical engineer. There he progressed into management where he held a number of supervisory positions and finally became Venture Manager for the Alkali Chemicals Division of FMC. Many of these ventures were overseas, including Germany, France, Spain, Italy, Turkey, Mexico, Venezuela, and Romania. In November 1985, after 38 years with FMC, Edward retired.

CAPTAIN
ROBERT M. GARCIA

TUCSON

Army Air Corps
Entered Service February 1942
Pilot P-47C and P-51B
318th Fighter Squadron, 325th Fighter Group
Mediterranean Theater, 15th Air Force
Distinguished Flying Cross, Air Medal with 4 OLC

Robert is a graduate of Tucson High School class of 1937. Convinced by his friend, John Madero, that conscription into the Army was imminent, he enlisted in the Air Corps soon after the Japanese attack at Pearl Harbor. Accepted as an aviation cadet for pilot training, he was sent to Santa Ana, California for preflight school. Primary flight school was completed at Cal-Aero in Ontario, California, where he trained and soloed on the PT-17 Stearman. The next phase, basic flight school, was at Lancaster, California, where he was introduced to the Vultee BT-13. Returning to his home state, Cadet Garcia trained on the AT-6 Texan and completed advanced flight school at Luke Field near Phoenix, where, in February 1943, he received his silver pilot wings and the gold bars of a newly commissioned second lieutenant.

Lt. Garcia in Italy, 1944 [1]

To begin the next phase of fighter pilot training, Robert was sent to the Southeast. He spent the next several months in the states of Tennessee, South Carolina and Florida learning and honing the skills necessary for combat. During this period he flew the Republic P-47 Thunderbolt, Douglas A-24 Dauntless and Curtis A-25 Helldiver. In October 1943 he departed Newport News, Virginia, by liberty ship for the Mediterranean Theater. After a one-month stopover in Casa Blanca he arrived in Italy and was assigned to the 325th Fighter Group stationed at Foggia in the southeast near the Adriatic Sea. From there and Lake Lesina, Robert flew fighter escort coverage for the 15th Air

---

1. Photos courtesy of Robert M. Garcia

Force B-17s and B-24s. Other missions included bombing and strafing military targets in support of Allied ground troops. He flew both the P-51 and P-47 with the "Checkertail Clan" over Italy, France, Germany, the Balkans including Yugoslavia, Hungary, Austria, Bulgaria, Czechoslovakia and Romania. He had three aerial victories (two Me-109s and one FW-190), but was officially credited with one victory and one probable.

During a dogfight over Hungary while on his 25th mission he took his P-47 into a high-speed dive that nearly cost him his life. The following press release describes this event of April 13, 1944:

> 15th Army Air Force—A P-47 Thunderbolt fighter pilot has experienced falling two miles at a speed faster than sound, and (an) additional three miles with his plane completely out of control, yet flew his crippled plane safely back to his base.
> The pilot, Lt. Robert M. Garcia (1122 No. Euclid Ave. Tucson, Arizona) was escorting heavy bombers over Budapest, Hungary. About 25 miles south of the city he became engaged in combat with an ME-109 at an altitude of 32,000 feet. The German plane went into a vertical dive. The Thunderbolt pilot followed, his plane in full "war boost" to get maximum speed. His shots hit the Jerry, causing it to explode.
> "I was traveling over 800 miles per hour. At that speed and altitude the controls wouldn't work. I was in what is called a 'compressibility dive'. At 18,000 feet I pulled out of the uncontrolled dive by using manual controls, but the plane went into a tight loop and I blacked out." He related.
> While Lt. Garcia was momentarily "blacked out" the plane went into a spin. A thick coating of frost formed on the interior of his cockpit canopy, obscuring his view. By instruments he saw that he was at 3,000 feet before he was successful in pulling out of the spin.
> Examination of his plane at his base revealed that the high-

speed descent had bulged the inspection plates, loosened rivets, and buckled the ailerons.

"I had given up all hope of coming out alive and was waiting for the crash," Lt. Garcia told intelligence Officers at interrogation. "I was surprisingly calm all the time."

In 1944 there was not much data available for flight surgeons concerning the effects on the human body during a high-speed pull-out. As a result, Robert was grounded for medical observation for a three-month period. He flew three more missions after returning to flying status and then was appointed Operations Officer for his squadron. Later, he was assigned to Headquarters of the 306th Fighter Wing as Assistant Officer (operations officer) and promoted to captain.

When the 325th Fighter Group returned to the US after VE Day, Captain Garcia and a few other pilots who had the option elected to transfer to the Pacific Theater where the war with Japan was not yet over. While enroute across the Atlantic heading for the Panama Canal, the war with Japan ended and his ship was diverted to Boston, Massachusetts.

Returning to civilian life, Robert went to work for the State of Arizona, Department of Employment Security Commission as a field advisor and payroll tax auditor. Later, he was office manager in the employer accounts office until his retirement in July 1978.

Mr. Garcia has three children and seven grandchildren.

FIRST LIEUTENANT GILBERT F. GONZALES

TUCSON

Army Air Corps
Entered Service in February 1943
Pilot of P-38 Lightning "Hija"
339th Fighter Squadron, 347th Fighter Group "Sunsetters"
Pacific Theater, 13th Air Force
Air medal with 1 OLC

Lt. Gonzales Returns From Pacific Duty

Tucsonian Was Member Of Squadron Which Shot Down 179 Planes

Back From War

First Lt. Gilbert F. Gonzales, son of Mrs. Delifina F. Moreno 526 South Herbert street, has returned to the United States having completed his tour of duty with the famed Sunsetters squadron of Brig. Gen. Earl W. Barnes' 13th air force fighter command.

During his Pacific tour, Lt. Gonzales piloted a P-38 Lightning fighter in air raids against the Japs from New Guinea through the Philippines and Borneo to the coast of French Indo-China and Singapore. His squadron is the top-scoring outfit in the jungle air force with 179 enemy planes destroyed in the air. He holds the Air Medal with one Oak Leaf cluster, the Asiatic-Pacific campaign ribbon with four battle stars and the Philippine Liberation ribbon with one star.

Lt. Gonzales was graduated from Tucson senior high school in 1938, and attended the University of Arizona. Before entering service he was a property clerk at Davis-Monthan field. His wife, the former Adeline Christine Morris, and two-year-old son, Gilbert M. Gonzales, live at 25 West Council street.

First Lt. Gilbert F. Gonzales, 25 West Council street, recently returned to the United States after participating as a P-38 Lightning fighter pilot in six raids against the Japs from New Guinea through the Philippines and Borneo to the coast of French Indo-China and Singapore. (U. S. Army photo)

This article appeared in the Arizona Daily Star in November 1945

Cadet Gonzales completed his primary pilot training at King City, California, and basic pilot training at Marana Field, Arizona. After receiving his gold bars and silver pilot wings at Williams Field, Arizona, in March 1944, Lt. Gonzales trained in P-39s at Moses Lake,

Wisconsin, and P-38s at Ontario, California. Called the "Fork-Tailed Devil" by the enemy, the Lockheed P-38 saw extensive service in the Pacific and other theaters. Considered one of the top fighter planes of its time, it had a speed of 400 mph and was armed with four 50 caliber machine guns and a 20mm cannon. Its twin engines gave the pilot an added measure of safety, acting as a buffer from enemy fire, and also gave this aircraft the ability to fly with only one engine. In December 1944, Gilbert was sent to the Southwest Pacific where he flew a P-38 on 62 combat missions totaling 318 hours in the cockpit. Some of these sorties included the bombing of Japanese oil production facilities in Borneo. He remembered that after long distance flights of 7 or 8 hours it was often necessary for ground crews to lift the stiff pilots out of their cockpits. [1]

Discharged from the service in January 1946, Gilbert returned to civilian life. In March 1951, during the Korean War, he was recalled to duty. When hostilities ended in 1953 he remained in the Air Force as a career officer rising to the rank of lieutenant colonel by the time of his retirement in 1977. His decorations and citations in addition to those listed in the news item above include the Meritorious Service Medal with two OLC, Air Force Commendation Medal, WW II Victory Medal, Air Force Longevity Medal with six OLC, National Defense Service Medal with bronze star, and the Air force Outstanding Unit Award.

Gilbert passed away in October 1994. He is survived by his wife Adeline, five children, fourteen grandchildren, and four great-grandchildren.

---

1. In the year before Lt. Gonzales was sent to the Pacific, the 339th squadron was already making a name for itself. On April 18th, 1943, P-38s of the 339th succeeded in their mission to intercept and destroy the aircraft carrying Admiral Isoroku Yamamoto. Yamamoto, best known for leading the attack on Pearl Harbor, was killed along with several other staff officers near Bougainville. John T. Wible describes the events of this mission in "The Yamamoto Mission".

STAFF SERGEANT
NICOLAS B. GUERRA

CLIFTON

Army Air Corps
Entered Service in August 1941
Gunner on B-24
431st Bomb Squadron, 11th Bomb Group
Pacific Theater, 7th Air Force
Distinguished Flying Cross with one Oak Leaf Cluster (2 DFC's)
Air Medal with 3 OLC

Entering the service three months prior to the Japanese attack on Pearl Harbor, Nick proceeded to Jefferson Barracks, Missouri, for basic training. Leaving Missouri for Texas, he spent the next several months on general duty at Kelly Field, Moore Field and Dalhart Field before completing Aerial Gunnery School at Harlingen Field. He then went to Wendover, Utah, where he completed advanced gunnery and fire control training before returning to his home state for combat crew training at Davis Monthon Field near Tucson. Advanced combat crew training was completed at Blythe Field, California, before he was sent to Lincoln, Nebraska, for final crew processing and assignment of a brand-new B-24 Liberator. In October 1943, Sgt Guerra and his crew departed Hamilton Field, California, heading to the South Pacific.

Sgt. Guerra and crewmembers on Tarawa Island in late 1943.[1] Back Row L to R: R. Bailey, W. Hogan, C. Mcgraw, F. Bloom, C. Luzon, R. Darley. Front Row L to R: N.Guerra, C. Sullivan, C. Melton.

From bases in the Ellice Island chain, Gilbert Island chain and Marshall Island chain, Nick flew 30 combat missions as a ball turret gunner.

In December 1944 Nick returned to the US and was stationed at Santa Ana Field (Calif.), Lowery Field (Colo.) and Amarillo Field (Tex.) before being discharged at Fort McArthur (Calif.) in September 1945. Back in civilian life he was rehired by the Phelps Dodge mining operation at Morenci where he was employed until his retirement in July 1981, with forty years of service.

Nicholas is married to the former Norberta Hernandez of Clifton. They have four children, seven grandchildren and four great-grandchildren.

---

1. Photos courtesy of Nicolas B. Guerra

STAFF SERGEANT
ALFRED L. HUISH JR

DOUGLAS

Army Air Corps
Aerial Photographer
722nd Bomb Squadron, 450th Bomb Group
Mediterranean Theater, 15th Air Force
Air Medal with 2 OLC, Purple Heart

Sgt. Huish was stationed in Italy with the 15th Air force. On July 27, 1944, while on his 30th mission as an aerial photographer, Sgt. Huish's B-24 was shot down by flak over Budapest, Hungary. Upon his parachute landing, he was taken prisoner and sent to a German hospital where he was treated for flak wounds and a dislocated shoulder. After two weeks in a Budapest prison, he was moved by rail to Stalag Luft 4 in Poland where he remained until February 6, 1945. With the Russian army advancing from the East, the Germans began marching thousands of Allied POWs to Stalag II-B, 400 miles away in Germany. Sgt. Huish hiked 53 nightmarish days in bitter cold, most of the time without enough food and water, and suffering from dysentery and frozen feet. About a week after arriving at Stalag II-B, Sgt Huish and two fellow POWs successfully escaped from the camp. Evading recapture for over a week, they wandered throughout the German countryside until being rescued by advancing British troops.[1][2][3]

Back in the States, Sgt.Huish was stationed near his home at Douglas Army Air Field when the war ended in September 1945.

---

1. Missing Aircrew Report #7198, National Archives, Suitland, Maryland
2. From story in Douglas Daily Dispatch dated August 26, 1945.
3. Photo is from story in Douglas Daily Dispatch dated August 26, 1945

LIEUTENANT HEBER M. HUISH

DOUGLAS

Army Air Corps
Pilot of P-51 Mustang
354th Fighter Squadron, 355th Fighter Group
European Theater, 8th Air Force

Heber is the brother of Alfred Huish (see page 91). Their mother, Trinidad A. Huish, was Hispanic. On July 7, 1944, while on a mission escorting heavy bombers, Heber was killed in action over Germany. First lieutenant Richard D. Cross, eyewitness to this event, stated, "a gaggle of bandits were attacking the big friends. Lt. Cross and Lt. Huish, flying wing, were following their leader who was making a pass at the attacking enemy aircraft. One of the German fighters was hit and as it blew apart, Lt. Huish's plane was struck by the debris and went into a spin".[1]

His death was strongly felt by 1st Lt. Louis Michelena (see page 119). They had become close friends when both trained together all through flight school.

---

1. Missing Aircrew Report #6794, National Archives, Suitland, Maryland.

STAFF SERGEANT
MANUEL H. LARINI

RAY/SONORA

Army Air Corps
Flight Engineer/Gunner on B-26 Marauder
497th Bomb Squadron, 344th Bomb Group
European Theater, 9th Air Force
Air Medal

On the morning of June 6, 1944 (D-Day), Sgt. Larini was killed off the coast of Montebourg, France, just minutes before American troops stormed ashore at Utah Beach. His B-26 Marauder was hit by enemy anti-aircraft fire as it approached the beach. The eyewitness account of Anthony J. Paulino, tail gunner on another plane, stated the following:

Right engine and forward bombay of plane was hit by flak, plane pulled left out of formation, three parachutes immediately left the ship from the rear. There was a fire in the forward bombay. I saw the plane explode approximately three and one half minutes after it left formation. Parachutes would have landed between a small island in the North Sea (probably meant English Channel) and mainland of France. At the time the chutes were descending there was a terrific tracer fire enemy ground opposition.[1]

There were no survivors. Sgt. Larini was 21 years old.[2]

The following letter was written to his mother Lupe just two days before he died.[3]

---

1. Missing Aircrew Report #5656, National Archives, Suitland, Maryland.
2. In the June/July 1994 issue of Air & Space magazine there is an excellent article by Daniel Ford titled "Did He Say Five Hundred Feet". Mr. Ford describes the events of that morning and how hundreds of B-26 Marauder bombers flew a low-level mission over Utah Beach. He mentions the 344th Bomb Group and their loss of a plane from flak. He goes on to say that out of some 290 Marauders from various groups, only one had been shot down over the beach. Could this have been Sgt. Larini's plane? I believe it was.
3. Photo and letter courtesy of Eva Kanouse.

Somewhere in England
June 4, 1944

Querida Madrecita,

Estas cuantas lineas para saludarle regandole a Dios que ustedes se encuentren bien. Yo estoy bien gracias a Dios.

El otro dia fui a Londres y me retrate. Cuando vaya devuelta los triago y se los mando. No he podido ir porque no puedo agarrar un pass. Aver cuando los puedo ir a traer.

Ayer Domingo fui a misa y me queria confesar pero no pude. Algun dia de estos se me consede confesarme.

Quisiera que Gabe se estubiera alla para que el me diga las nuevas. Pero ahora yo creo que el tambien le van a tener que decir las nuevas de el pueblo.

Hoy recibi un paquete de dulces que me mando la Prieta. Los que mando usted, todavia no los he recibido. Qualquier dia de estos los agarro.

Bueno yo creo que sera todo para esta ves. Saludeme a los tios, primos, Ramon, mi Nana, Padilla, Guero, y usted y mis hermanas reciben todo mi carino. Este es su hijo que nunca los olvida.

Manuel Larini

P.S. Ya subi a el otro grado mas alto.

SERGEANT HENRY L. LEYVA

TUCSON

Army Air Corps
Entered Service February 1944
Radio Operator/Gunner on B-24

A member of the Enlisted Reserve while still a high school student, Henry entered active service soon after his graduation from Tucson High in January 1944. He completed radio school at Scott Field, Illinois and then returned to Arizona for gunnery school at Yuma. Joining up with a combat crew in Lemoore, California, he proceeded to Walla Walla, Washington for combat crew training. By this time the war in Europe was going well for the Allies, so his crew-training phase was extended. Enjoying this period of duty, he logged many flight hours on patrol along the Pacific Coast searching for Japanese balloons. As Henry states "I flew 100 missions in the Battle of Walla Walla".

In the summer of 1945, he and his crew were at Merced, California, where they were issued a new B-24 Liberator. One week before their scheduled flight to the Philippines, the war ended. He was then assigned to Mountain Home Field near Boise, Idaho, and later at a radar outpost at Half Moon Bay south of San Francisco, before being discharged in May 1946.

Back in civilian life, Henry worked for 15 years as deputy treasurer of Pima County. He obtained a BS and BA degree from the University of Arizona majoring in accounting. He has held the position of controller for several Tucson firms and was a licensed Public Accountant.

Henry married Fresia Sotomayor Felix in June 1948. They have four children, nine grandchildren, and two great-grandchildren.

Sgt. Leyva with members of his crew. He is in the front row, 4th from left.[1]

---

1. Photo courtesy of Henry L. Leyva

FIRST LIEUTENANT ORLANDO LOERA

MIAMI/MESA

Army Air Corps
Bombardier on B-25
484th Bomb Squadron, 340th Bomb Group
Mediterranean Theater, 12th Air Force
Air Medal with OLC

On September 9, 1943, Lt. Loera was killed while taking part in a night mission from Cantania Main Airdrome in Sicily.[1] He was 24 years old. Orlando was a graduate of Mesa High School class of 1937 and Arizona State Teachers College (now ASU) class of 1941. He was on the varsity tennis teams at both schools.[2]

---

1. Missing Aircrew Report #3686, National Archives, Suitland, Maryland.
2. Mesa High School yearbook 1937, "The Superstition" and Arizona State College yearbook 1940, "The Sahuaro".

STAFF SERGEANT
FRANK G. MABANTE

NOGALES

Army Air Corps
Entered Service November 1941
Gunner on B-17F
525th Bomb Squadron, 379th Bomb Group
European Theater, 8th Air Force
Air Medal with 1 OLC

Frank was a graduate of Nogales High School class of 1938. In late 1941, just prior to the Japanese attack at Pearl Harbor, he enlisted in the Air Corps. From the reception center at St. Louis, Missouri he was sent to Lowery Field, Colorado for aircraft armament training, and later to Las Vegas, Nevada for gunnery school. It was there in August 1942 that he received his wings as an aerial gunner. He remained in Las Vegas as a gunnery instructor before being assigned to Williams Field, Arizona. Being stationed in his home state had its advantages (just a few hours away from mom's cooking), but he was also anxious to join the action overseas. His younger brother James, soon to become an aerial gunner, was already stationed in North Africa. Frank performed the routine duties of arming and bore sighting AT-6s and P-38s for student pilots at Williams until finally receiving orders for combat crew training. For the next several months he trained on B-17s at Peyote, Texas, Dyersburg, Tennessee, and Salina, Kansas. On November 2, 1943, he boarded the HMS Queen Elizabeth in New York and sailed for England.

Assigned to the 8th Air Force, 379th Bomb Group, 525th Bomb Squadron, stationed at Kimbolton (about 45 miles North of London), Sergeant Mabante began flying combat missions to Germany. On January 29, 1944, while on his sixth mission, his Flying Fortress was shot down and he was taken prisoner. He spent the next fourteen and a half months in German POW camps Stalag Luft IV and Stalag Luft VI.

The following account describes the tense moments on this final and most unforgettable mission:

As we approached our target at Frankfurt A/M, one of our engines started faltering. Then as we dropped our bomb load we lost another one. With only two engines left we were unable to keep up with the formation and soon were being pursued by enemy aircraft. One of our remaining engines was hit but we were able to survive the final attack because of the heavy cloud cover. As luck would have it our single engine was not delivering full power and we were steadily losing altitude. Hoping we could reach the English Channel and ditch, our pilot ordered us to dump anything out to lighten the ship. This included ammunition, bags with our flying gear, vacuum bottles, radio equipment etc.. Soon it was apparent this was not going to work and the order to "bail out" came via the intercom. From my tail gun position I could see the crew begin to exit the aircraft while I changed into my army shoes. I didn't want to jump with my sheep lined boots for I knew they would fly off in the slipstream. Going out the side door I waited until I had cleared the horizontal stabilizer before pulling my ripcord. My chute opened and immediately I was below the clouds and heading for some trees. I was surprised at how low of an altitude we had jumped. From my vantage point as I descended, I saw our B-17 for the last time about a half mile ahead as it made a banked turn to the right and disappeared in some low clouds. There were tears in my eyes as I saluted "The Queen of the Skies" for bringing us this far. Landing in a tree I began to free myself from the chute harness. As I unbuckled the last leg strap, I dropped like a sack of potatoes from a height of 18 to 20 feet. My feet and ankles ached as I struggled to get up. Within seconds I was surrounded by "Deutsche Soldaten" pointing menacing weapons toward me. One of them hollered "pistole, pistole?" I replied "nein, nein!" I was escorted to a dirt road to where a "Kommandant Officer" and non-coms were waiting. There were some civilians there too. A priest among them got as close as he could to listen to the interrogation. Our eyes met and he flashed me the victory sign. I was taken to a building and locked up alone. I still did not know what had happened to any of my fellow crewmembers. Later on that evening I was shown some photos of our B-17 against a clump of trees. A second photo showed that the tail gunner's two inch thick armored glass was full of holes. I had always been told it was bulletproof. I suspected that the Wehrmacht had done some close range target practice earlier that day.

Frank was interned for six months at Stalag Luft VI at Heydekrug (Lithuania) before being sent to Stalag Luft IV at Kiefheide near the Baltic Sea. Music was one form of entertainment enjoyed by the POWs. With the help of the Red Cross, musical instruments were provided (Frank played guitar), and a band was formed called the "Hot Tamales". In early February 1945, the camp was vacated by the Germans and he was put on a forced march to the west that lasted over two months and covered approximately 500 miles. He weighed close to 100 pounds when he was liberated by British reconnaissance troops on April 15, 1945.[1]

Returning to civilian life, Frank went to work for Allison Steel (later Marathon Steel) in Phoenix. He retired from there after thirty-eight years of service. Also in the years following his separation from the military, Frank obtained a private pilot's license, and flying became one of his favorite hobbies.

In October 1999 Frank passed away after an extended illness. He is survived by his wife Alice, three children, nine grandchildren, and three great-grandchildren.

---

1. Information about Stalag Luft IV and the forced death march can be obtained on the internet by entering the keyword Stalag Luft IV. Several Web sites will be listed providing written accounts by POWs who survived the march.

Sgt. Mabante and fellow crewmembers. [2]
Back Row L to R: J. Dennis, J. Rhyner, L. Levens, H. Walz.
Front Row L to R: G. Ventimigalia, F. Mabante, L. Giles, M. Eckleberry,
O. Hughes, J. Ault.

---

2. All photos courtesy of Frank G. Mabante.

STAFF SERGEANT
JAMES A. MABANTE

NOGALES

Army Air Corps
Entered Service in June 1942
Gunner on B-17F
384th Bomb Squadron, 99th Bomb Group
Mediterranean Theater 15th Air Force
Air Medal with 4 OLC

Sergeant James Mabante was killed on December 19, 1943 when his B-17 Flying Fortress was shot down by enemy aircraft while, on a bombing mission to Austria. His plane crashed about 40 miles south of Innsbruck on the return leg to his home base in Italy.[1] The veteran waist gunner had seen combat in the North African, Sicilian and Italian campaigns, and was on his 49th mission. He would have been transferring back to the States upon completing 50 missions.

James was a 1940 graduate of Nogales High School. He first enlisted in the Air Corps as a ground crewmember, but later while in North Africa volunteered for flight duty as a waist gunner.[2]

Sergeant James Mabante is buried at the Nogales city cemetery. He is the younger brother of Sgt. Frank Mabante (see page 103) who spent 14 ½ months as a POW when his B-17 was shot down in January 1944.

1. Missing Aircrew Report #1527, National Archives, Suitland, Maryland.
2. Photo courtesy of Alice Mabante

FLIGHT OFFICER JUAN S. MADERO

TUCSON

Army Air Corps
Pilot on B-25

Juan was a graduate of Tucson High School class of 1937. He also attended the University of Arizona. Accepted for pilot training early in the war, it wasn't until 1944 that Juan became a cadet. The delay was the result of difficulties he experienced due to his foreign birth (born in Cananea, Sonora, Mexico). In June 1944 he completed preflight school at Kansas State College in Emporia Kansas. It is not known where he was sent for primary and basic flight school, but advanced training was at Douglas Army Air Field in Arizona where he received his wings in June, 1945. On August 15, 1945, while stationed at Yuma Army Air Field, Juan died in a plane crash.[1]

---

1. Photo courtesy of Robert Madero

The following news item appeared in the Douglas Daily Dispatch on August 16, 1945.

Five Yuma Fliers Killed in Crash

YUMA (P)—Five members of the Yuma army air field flying personnel died in the crash of a B-25 bomber on Powell peak, southeast of Topock, during a combat training mission Saturday, army authorities disclosed here Wednesday.

Among those killed were twin brothers, Second Lieuts. William G. Winter and John R. Winter, 20 years old, of Towanda, Pa.

The other victims were:

Lt. Robert L. Laird, 21 years old, of Laredo, Texas, whose father, Col. John A. Laird, is attached to the 801th specialized depot, Buffalo, N. Y. Young Laird was pilot of the aircraft.

Flight Officer Juan S. Madero, Jr., 26-year-old son of Juan Madero, of Tucson. He was co-pilot. His widow, Jennie V. Madero, lives at 144 South Main street, Tucson.

Pfc. William F. Strange, 24 years old, of Rockmart, Ga., radio operator.

ARM2/c
ALBERT E. MADRID

CLIFTON

US Navy
Entered Service August 1942
Radioman/Gunner on SBD Dauntless, SB2C Helldiver and PB4Y Liberator
Bombing Squadrons VB-16, VB19 and PBS-200
Pacific Theater aboard USS Enterprise and USS Lexington
Two Distinguished Flying Crosses, three Air Medals

Albert is a graduate of Clifton High School class of 1939. Entering the Navy in the summer of 1942, he completed basic training at San Diego and advanced training as an Aviation Radio-Operator/Gunner at Miami, Florida in Oct. 1943. During the two years that followed he served three separate combat tours in the Pacific, where he completed a total of 96 missions. On his first tour he flew on SBD Dauntless dive bombers off the aircraft carrier "Enterprise", or Big "E" as she was affectionately known.

On Albert's second tour he was assigned to the carrier "Lexington" where he flew on Curtiss SB2C Helldivers. Returning to the South Pacific for his third tour, he flew in PB4Y Liberators where he completed his final missions on patrol. His decorations include two Distinguished Flying Crosses, three Air Medals, Presidential Unit Citations, Good Conduct Medal, American Theater of War Medal, WWII Victory Medal and campaign medals for Midway, Guam, Gilberts, Marshalls, Palau, Philippines, China, Okinawa, Formosa, Iwo Jima, Chichi Jima, Ryuko, Nansi Shoto and finally Japan.

Experiencing many nightmarish moments in combat and having lived through some of the most intense naval battles of the Pacific exacted a toll on Albert's health. One month after his discharge from the Navy in September 1945, he ended up in a VA hospital with what they labeled as a "War Psychosis". As Albert states this was a nice word for "crazy". During the next 15 years he was in and out of the hospital for short and long stays, suffering from comas to outright dementia. Through psychology, psychoanalysis and strong drugs as medication, he was finally cured when many thought it was not possible. He resided in Los Angeles, California until his death in 1991.

ARM2c Albert Madrid on the wing of Curtiss SB2C Helldiver in Jan, 1944. Pilot is Lt. Koch.[1]

---

1. Photo courtesy of Albert E. Madrid.

WARRANT OFFICER EUGENE A. MARIN

WINKLEMAN

Army Air Corps
Entered Service March 1943
Navigator

Eugene is a graduate of Hayden High School class of 1941. His thirty-three months of service were spent stateside at training facilities in California, Idaho, Massachusetts, and Texas. He completed basic training, radio operator school and gunnery school before receiving his navigator wings at San Marcos, Texas in December 1944.

Returning to civilian life after his discharge in December 1945, Gene took advantage of the "GI Bill" and enrolled at Arizona State Teachers College (now Arizona State University). Obtaining a bachelor's degree in 1949, and a master's degree in 1954, he taught for 16 years in the Phoenix schools and for two years in the Calexico (California) school system. He then joined the Office Of Economic Opportunity as a director until 1971. The following year, he earned a PhD from United States International University, and accepted a position as director of student financial aid at ASU. From 1981 until his retirement in 1983, he was with the U.S. Department of Education in Washington D.C. Mr. Marin resided in Phoenix until his death in November, 1999. He is survived by his wife Marie, two children, and five grandchildren.

ENSIGN
ALFRED C. MARQUEZ

HAYDEN

US Navy
Entered Service 1942
Flight Instructor

Alfred is a graduate of Hayden High School class of 1941. Entering the Navy, he was selected for pilot training where he learned to fly the NP-1 Spartan, N2ST3 Stearman and Vultee type aircraft. He was sent to Corpus Christi, Texas for advanced flight school. There, at the completion of training on the North American SNJ "Texan", Alfred received the gold bar and wings of a naval aviator. Ensign Marquez was then sent to instrument flight school in Atlanta, Georgia. Upon completion, Alfred served as a flight instructor in Beeville, and Kingsville, Texas until his discharge from the Navy in 1945.[1]

1. Photo courtesy of Alfred C. Marquez

Returning to civilian life, Alfred took advantage of the GI Bill and enrolled at Arizona State College (now Arizona State University). In September 1946 he transferred to the University of Arizona where he graduated in 1948 with a BA degree in Economics. After entering Law School at the U of A and earning his LLB there in 1950, he went to work in the Attorney General's Office for the State of Arizona. His next position was as deputy county attorney for Pima County. In 1955 Alfred became administrative assistant to Congressman Stewart Udall. After a short period as a prosecutor for the City of Tucson, he entered private practice in 1956. Becoming a founding partner in the Tucson law firm of Mesch, Marquez and Rothschild, Alfred practiced law until July 1980 when President Jimmy Carter appointed him U.S. District Judge. In July 1991 Judge Marquez retired from the bench.

FIRST LIEUTENANT RALPH LOUIS MICHELENA

SOLOMONVILLE

Army Air Corps
Entered Service in October 1942
Pilot of P-51D Mustang "Arizona Bronco" and "Arizona Bronco II"
358th Fighter Squadron, 355th Fighter Group
European Theater 8th Air Force
Distinguished Flying Cross, Air Medal with 6 OLC

A member of an eastern Arizona pioneer family, Louis was raised in Ray/Sonora and Solomonville. In 1941 he graduated from Safford High School and subsequently enrolled at Gila Junior College (now Eastern Arizona College). During his freshmen year he began taking flying lessons through the Civilian Pilot Training Program (CPTP) where he soloed on a Piper J-3 Cub. In June 1942 he graduated from the CPTP and soon after obtained his private pilot's license.

Knowing that his draft number would be drawn soon, Louis enlisted in the Army Air Corps in October 1942. After basic training he was assigned to Bullman Field, Kentucky, and Lawson Field, Georgia, as a court reporter. Learning that Louis already had a pilot's license, his commanding officer encouraged him to apply for entry into the aviation cadet program. On January 1, 1943, he began preflight school at Maxwell Field, Alabama.

After two months of preflight, he was sent to Lakeland Field, Florida for primary flight training. There he learned to fly Stearman PT-17s. His next phase, basic flight training, was at Courtland Field, Alabama, where he flew Vultee BT-13s. The final phase, advanced flight training, was at Craig Field, Alabama where he flew the North American AT-6 Texan and Curtiss P-40. It was at Craig Field on November 3, 1943 that Louis received his silver pilot wings and commission as a 2nd lieutenant.

After graduating from flight school, Lt. Michelena continued to train on Bell P-39s and Republic P-47s until receiving his orders to the European Theater of Operations. Departing New York on the New Amsterdam in April 1944, the Atlantic crossing took several days before arriving in Glasgow, Scotland. Soon after his arrival, Louis began pre-combat training on the North American P-51 B Mustang. Upon completion, he was assigned to the 355th Fighter Group, 358th Fighter Squadron stationed in Steeple Morden about 30 miles north of London.

The primary mission of the 355th Fighter Group was to escort the heavy bomber squadrons of B-17s and B-24s to and from their long-range targets on the European continent. They also destroyed targets in support of the invasion (D-Day June 6, 1944) and the ground offensive which followed. Louis flew missions in support of the the campaigns in Normandy, Northern France, Southern France, the Ardennes and the Far East (Russia). Many of these missions required that they strafe ememy positions, airdromes, railroads and other tactical targets, putting the pilot at greater risk of being shot down by small arms fire. On one mission Louis was shot down and captured by the Germans. While he was being moved to a central prison camp, he and several others escaped. He was able to evade recapture and with help from the *Maquis* (French Underground), returned to his unit in England.

On one mission in September 1944 code-named "Frantic Seven", he participated in the escort of over 100 heavy bombers to Warsaw,

Poland and then on to Russia where they landed. But unlike other missions, these B-17s were carrying supplies to be dropped to the Polish Underground who were surrounded by German troops. In a dogfight with German aircraft attacking the bombers, Michelena was credited with shooting down one Me-109, and damaging another. On their departure from Russia, they escorted the bombers to bomb a marshalling yard at Szolnok, Hungry, before returning to England via Italy.

Lt. Louis Michelena inEngland, 1944 [1]

For his role in "Frantic-7", Louis was awarded the Distinguished Cross of Valor by the Polish government in ceremonies 50 years later aboard the Aircraft Carrier Intrepid in New York harbor. In the fall of 1995, for his efforts beyond Frantic-7, the Russian Government presented him the commemorative medal "The 50th Anniversary of the Victory in the Great Patriotic War" (World War II).

---

1. Photo courtesy of Louis Michelena

In his role as a P-51 pilot, Louis flew 55 combat missions for a total of 271 hours in the air. He destroyed 11 enemy aircraft, 2 of which were aerial victories, and damaged 2 more.

Returning to the States in the fall of 1944, Louis married his high school sweetheart, Carolyn Garcia, of Buena Vista (near Safford). He spent the remainder of the war as a gunnery instructor at Las Vegas Field, Nevada, and flight instructor at Marana Field, Arizona. In October 1945 he was discharged from the service and returned home to Solomonville. During the next few years he operated a grocery store and was elected Justice of the Peace in Graham County.

In May of 1951, during the Korean War, he was recalled to active duty. After training on KB-29s at Davis Monthan Air Force Base in Tucson, Louis served two tours in the Pacific. He was promoted to captain and flew as aircraft commander. In addition to the medals mentioned above, his decorations include the Good Conduct Medal, WWII Victory Medal, American Campaign Medal and the EAME Ribbon.

After the war, he returned once again to civilian life in Arizona. From 1965 to 1966 he was an aide to Governor Sam Goddard as Director of Manpower. Later he held various administrative positions with the city, county and federal governments in areas related to equal employment opportunities for minorities. In 1984, after serving as a Supervisor of Investigation with the Equal Employment Opportunity Commission, Louis retired from civil service.

Louis and his wife reside in Tempe, Arizona They have three children, six grandchildren and four great-grandchildren.

CAPTAIN RAYMOND N. MORAGA

TEMPE

Army Air Corps
Entered Service in 1940
Pilot of P-47 "Miss Champayne"
386th Fighter Squadron, 365th Fighter Bomber Group "Hell Hawks"
European Theater, 9th Air Force
Air Medal with sixteen OLC

Raymond was a graduate of Tempe High School class of 1937. He attended Arizona State Teachers College (now Arizona State University) and was a member of the Arizona National Guard 158th Infantry Regiment (Later to be known as Bushmasters). He transferred to the Army Air Corps and began pilot preflight training at San Antonio, Texas in the fall of 1942. He received his wings and commission in Waco, Texas in May of 1943.

By the spring of 1944, Lieutenant Moraga was a P-47 Thunderbolt pilot with the 9th Air Force stationed in England. Fighter squadrons of the 9th had been moved from North Africa to England in the months prior to the Allied invasion of Europe. Under the command of General E. R. Quesada, the primary mission of the 9th AF at this stage in the war was as a tactical force to destroy bridges, roads and railways leading to Normandy on the coast of France. They also attacked airdromes and troop movements and escorted bombers.

Compressibility was an unexplained phenomenon experienced by many P-47 fighter pilots while in a super high-speed dive. This condition is characterized by complete loss of elevator control when attempting to pull out of the dive. The following report was written by Tom Leonard, technical representative for Republic Aviation, the builders of the P-47. In the document he reports to his management what Lt. Col.

Coffey, Capt. Murphy and Lt. Moraga experienced while in a compressibility dive and how they survived it. [1] [2]

---

1. Photo and technical report courtesy of Ernest Moraga
2. Note: Lt Col. Robert L. Coffey, the group leader mentioned in this report was credited with six aerial victories during WWII. At the time that Raymond was flying as his wingman, Coffey was still two victories short of the five required for Ace. In late June and early July, 1944 he picked up three more. This must have been a good reason to celebrate since there were not many Aces in the 9th AF. The opportunities to mix it up with the Jerries in aerial combat just didn't exist in the 9th like they did in the 8th AF.
   When I begin doing research on Moraga in the late 1980's, I wanted to talk to someone who had been in his unit. I learned that Coffey was from Johnstown, Pennsylvania, so I started calling numbers listed for that name in the Johnstown phone directory. Was I surprised when the weak sounding voice I was talking to turned out to be Col. Coffey's mother who was in her 90's. She was a sweet, friendly lady and talked my ear off about the war, her children, and how she might be moving to Florida in the future. It was from her that I sadly learned that her son, who had remained in the service after the war, had been killed in a jet plane crash in 1949.

REPUBLIC AVIATION REPRESENTATIVE
EUROPEAN THEATER OF OPERATIONS
AAF STATION 406

23 April 1944.

SUBJECT: Compressibility Dives of Lt. Col. Robert L. Coffey, Captain John R. Murphy, Lt. Raymond M. Moraga.

TO : Mr. Prescott Morris Smith,
Administrative Liaison Representative
Republic Aviation Corp.

Lt. Col. Robert L. Coffey, Jr.

On 13 April 1944 Lt. Col. Bob Coffey was leading the 365th Fighter Group on a bomber escort mission. He was flying a D-20 model airplane number 42-76518 at 24,000 feet when a superior force of enemy fighters dove through the overcast on the bombers. He turned into the attack chandelling to 26,000 feet and came in on the tail of the Jerries.

The majority of the enemy broke and dove for the deck; however, he was able to close to within 400 yards of one ME-109. He was using full throttle and water injection to close, with an estimated 64 inches of mercury. He fired at the enemy aircraft and observed several strikes before the Jerry did a wing-over and dove for the deck.

Col. Coffey followed the e/a in a vertical spiralling dive. He gave the e/a several bursts during the dive. He was still using full throttle and water injection. He followed the e/a in this maneuver until approximately 15,000 feet when the Jerry lost control and the e/a started flicking violently. Col. Coffey then started to over-run the e/a. He retarded his throttle and lost control.

Col. Coffey estimates he was doing well over 500 MPH around 15,000 feet when he retarded his throttle. He is not too sure of these figures as he was intent on closing on the e/a. He lost all stick control and experienced extreme aileron buffetting. He gave it full throttle and water injection and used both hands on the stick in an attempt to regain control.

He took one turn on his elevator trim control. He managed to get a little control and came out of the dive on the deck zooming vertically back to 10,000 feet.

His canopy had frosted completely over. He opened his canopy and the frost cleared away. He did not fire his guns during his recovery from the dive.

He was able to stop his zoom and level off at 10,000 feet. He was still indicating 200 MPH when he leveled out. He does not recall his airspeed exactly. He looked at it during his dive and stated it was such a fantastic figure he did not believe the gauge. As he recalls it, it was over 700 MPH which was probably around 10,000 feet. This makes it at least 825 MPH not correcting for the airspeed gauge being slow.

The right aileron was torn half off. The outer half having left the plane completely. Col. Coffey did not know this had happened until he noticed it during his zoom. The left aileron, while intact, looked strained having an oil can in back of the center hinge on the bottom surface, also two slight wrinkles. The rest of the plane checked out OK and two new ailerons were installed. Pictures of the torn aileron are attached. The torn aileron is accompanying this report.

Capt. John R. Murphy

Capt. John Murphy was leading the 388th Squadron on this mission. He was on the right of Col. Coffey in airplane number 42-75689. He noticed the enemy fighters

CAPTAIN RAYMOND N. MORAGA

diving on the bombers and climbed to intercept them. He estimates he got a little above Col. Coffey and to his left as they closed on the Jerries. All but one of the e/a flicked down as they closed; this being the one Col. Coffey fired at.

Capt. Murphy was using full throttle and water injection as he was closing. Col. Coffey fired and the e/a dove for the deck, Col. Coffey and his wing man, Lt. Moraga, after it. Since there had been over 100 e/a in the group attacking the bombers, Capt. Murphy dove also to give cover in case a trap awaited below.

He entered his dive by split S-ing. In order to observe what was happening ahead he flew upside down about 120° in a 60° dive after Col. Coffey. He maintained full throttle and water injection which he did not retard during the dive. He did not note his manifold pressure but imagines it was high.

At about 20,000 feet he rolled and righted himself still maintaining his dive which had steepened. He remembers his air speed as being over the red line, 500 MPH, at this time and increasing.

The nose of his plane started dropping towards vertical and beyond. He could not prevent it from assuming a vertical dive and had to take 3 turns on his elevator trim tabs to keep it from going past the vertical position.

He had aileron control which he did not use; however, he experienced no buffeting. His elevator control was frozen and he could not budge it although he used both hands and pulled as hard as he could. He was getting very low very fast, and very worried.

He started to come out and removed the trim. He is not sure he removed all the trim. He zoomed to 8,000 feet before he could stop this zoom.

He came out of his dive suddenly describing it as having no control and suddenly having control, which phenomena seems to accompany the firing of the guns. Capt. Murphy does not recall firing his guns; however, he had fired them. Very possibly he fired them as he was pulling to recover from the dive. He had his gun switch on.

The windshield frosted over so he could not see out. He did not use the defroster or open the canopy. He wiped the glass with his hands and managed to maintain limited visibility. His canopy did not completely clear off until after his zoom.

There was no damage to Capt. Murphy's plane.

Lt. Raymond N. Moraga

Lt. Ray Moraga was flying Col. Coffey's wing in plane number 42-76593. When Col. Coffey chandelled up after the Jerries, Lt. Moraga chandelled with Col. Coffey and maintained his position with him. He had to use full throttle and water injection to keep up. When Col. Coffey dove after the Jerry, Lt. Moraga followed, still using full throttle and water injection which he did not retard during the dive.

At approximately 20,000 feet he noticed Col. Coffey drifting away from him. The e/a was still going straight down so he took two bursts at the Jerry.

He estimates it was about this time that he went into compressibility. He had been in a compressibility dive before and he was not worried about himself yet, but was still concentrating on the e/a he was following.

He fired two more bursts he estimates about 15,000 feet in hopes of hitting the Jerry who was still going straight down, buffetting badly, and he estimates out of control.

He was still going straight down. He experienced no buffetting but his canopy started to cloud over. He now started to worry about himself and tried to pull out but he could not budge his controls. He could see the trees below him and they were getting closer fast.

He now became very worried and considered jumping but knew this was impossible so concentrated on pulling it out. He had been told by a Republic Representative in the States not to use any trim to recover from compressibility so he didn't take any.

He was using two hands and pulling when he accidentally fired his guns. It was at this instant or immediately after, he does not recall which as he did not pay too much attention to the firing of his guns, that his plane caught hold and started out.

He practically came out on instruments as his canopy had frosted over completely. He opened his canopy three holes and it immediately cleared off. He was then above the tree tops and going like hell. He pulled the stick back and zoomed to 10,000 feet.

He apparently came out in an arc without a zoom as he didn't use any trim to recover from the dive. This is one point I would like cleared up as all previous cases the pilot has taken trim as instructed by Joe Parker and others. I fully realize it is not our job to tell the pilots how to fly but there should be one system of coming out of a compressibility dive and that one should be the best. Where the pilot uses no trim and comes out in an arc, the tail of the arc can get very low when he is coming out on the deck.

There was no major damage to Lt. Moraga's plane. The front part of the right wing shackel was bent and a new part installed, everything else checked out OK.

Suggestions

Again the subject of firing the guns to recover from a compressibility dive becomes apparent. This phenomena was mentioned in my report of 4 July 1943. I am attaching for further reference a carbon copy of this report.

I recommend tests be run on this phenomena and that this information, if verified, be given to all P-47 pilots as it seems several have gone in from a high speed dive over enemy territory. If firing the guns is an answer or a help it should at least be tried.

Several reports, such as mentioned in my report of 17 October, in which Lt. Leack, who had experienced compressibility before and in a much worse dive recovered immediately and with no damage to the plane simply by firing his guns, seem to verify this.

Firing the guns would create a turbulence at the nozzel and through the entire cone of fire to the conversion point. At the speed of the plane, this cone of created turbulence would be rapidly traversed by the P-47 and some of it possibly cause a slight break in the compressibility air flow over the elevators. This might cause only a momentary freeing or lessening of the elevator pressure. The pilot is exerting extreme stick pressure at this time so any momentary lessening of the elevator pressure would enable him to obtain some stick control and start his recovery. While this is merely surmise, it seems very probable.

If these tests prove what is suspected, this would help to eliminate the dangers resulting from a compressibility dive over enemy territory. If the air flow over the elevators is unchanged by the firing, the slowing down of the plane due to the recoil would seem reason enough to shoot some ammunition at the enemy.

It would definitely be a morale booster if the pilot knew he had an ace in the hole to help his recovery from a compressibility dive. And it would improve the attitude of some pilots who hesitate to dive straight down for fear of running into compressibility.

Tom Leonard
Technical Representative
Republic Aviation Corp.

- 3 -

Raymond Moraga Funeral Saturday

Requiem high mass for Captain Raymond N. Moraga will be conducted at 10 o'clock Saturday morning from Our Lady of Mount Carmel church. The Rev. Paul G. Lawrence will officate.

Rosary will be said Friday evening at 8 o'clock at the Carr Mortuary chapel. Interment will be in St. Francis cemetery, Phoenix. Thunderbird Legion Post, No. 41, of Phoenix, will conduct military graveside rites.

Captain Moraga, son of Mr. and Mrs. Carmen Moraga, 901 Dorsey Lane, was killed in air combat over France, June 10, 1944.

He was a graduate of Tempe High school and had attended Arizona State college. He entered military service with the Arizona National Guard in September, 1940. He was 25 years old at the time of his death.

Survivors, in addition to his parents, are five brothers and two sisters.

Four days after D-day on June 10, 1944, Raymond was reported missing in action while on a mission over Normandy. Confirmation of his death occurred the following year. In April 1949, at the request of his family, his body was returned from Europe. This news item appeared on the front page of the Tempe Daily News on April 29, 1949.

LIEUTENANT RAYMOND B. MORALES

PHOENIX

Army Air Corps
Entered Service November 1942
Instructor Pilot in "Zone of Fort"

After completing preflight training at Orange County Airport Cadet Center (Calif.) in 1943, Raymond was sent to Morton Air Academy in Blythe, California, for primary training on Fairchild PT-19s. He then returned to Arizona at Marana Field near Tucson, for basic training on Stearman BT-13s. Advanced flight training was at Luke Field near his hometown of Phoenix. It was there in April 1944, after completing training on AT-6s, that he was awarded silver wings and received his commission. Over the next 16 months, Raymond was stationed in Nevada as a pilot/gunnery instructor. During this period he flew P-39s, P-63s, B-26s and B-17s. Raymond remained in the service after the war ended in August 1945.

For the next five years Raymond was assigned to reserve duty at Davis Monthan and Williams Air Force Base in Arizona. With the beginning of hostilities in Korea, he became a flight instructor on T-28s and on the Air Force's first generation jet trainer, the T-33.

Lt. Ray Morales, Indian Springs, Nevada, June 1944 [1]

While at Williams he performed simultaneous duty as a civilian pilot instructor with Phoenix College/Phoenix Union High School District "Air Age" program. Assigned overseas, Raymond flew F-86 Sabre jets while stationed with the 36th Fighter Bomber Wing at Suwan, Korea and Itazuke, Japan. Other types of aircraft Raymond flew while in the Air Force included the F-80, F-89, F-101, C-47 and B-57. Some of his non-flight duties were Engineering Officer, Material

---

1. Photo courtesy of Raymond B. Morales

Officer, Air Base Commander, Maintenance advisor to the Philippine Airforce, Chief of Maintenance, and Chief of Material.

Retiring in June of 1970 with the rank of lieutenant colonel, Raymond had completed almost 28 years of service. His career had spanned three wars-World War II, Korea and Vietnam. His decorations include the Meritorious Service Medal, Air Force Commendation Medal with OLC, and the Korean UN Service Medal.

TECHNICAL SERGEANT CHARLES P. NAVARRO

PHOENIX

Army Air Corps
Flight Engineer/Gunner on B-17G
840th Bomb Squadron, 483rd Bomb Group
Mediterranean Theater, 15th Air Force
Air Medal with OLC

On July 15, 1944 while on his 31st mission, Sergeant Navarro was killed when his aircraft crashed into the Adriatic Sea. His flak-damaged B-17 Flying Fortress was returning to Sterparone, Italy from a bombing mission to the Ploesti oil refineries in Romania. An air sea rescue was conducted but to no avail.[1] He was 21 years old.

---

1. Missing Aircrew Report #6955, National Archives, Suitland, Maryland.

TECHNICAL SERGEANT RAUL A. NEGRETTE

WILLIAMS

Army Air Corps
Entered Service in January 1943
Radio Operator/Gunner on B-24 "Ye Olde Battle Ax"
705th Bomb Squadron, 446th Bomb Group
European Theater, 8th Air Force
Air Medal with 2 OLC

Raul is a graduate of Williams High School class of 1940. He was attending Arizona State College in Flagstaff (now NAU) prior to entering the Air Corps in early 1943. He completed radio operator school at Sioux Falls, South Dakota and aerial gunnery school at Yuma before being sent overseas in January 1945. Assigned to the 446th Bomb Group with the 8th Air Force stationed at Bungay, England, Raul began flying combat missions to strategic targets in Germany. Raul states:

> *One mission I remember particularly was an attack we made on Kiel, the German submarine base. We were hit by flak and one engine began smoking. Our pilot asked for permission to leave the formation after dropping our bomb load—of course, it was granted. Our aircraft was forced to fly slower and at a lower altitude. We were forced to drop equipment to lighten our load as we managed to limp across the English Channel. The White Cliffs of*

Dover never looked better as we managed to land at Bungay engine off, prop feathered. On landing we discovered we had no brakes on one side. Our pilots, 1st Lt. Arden M. Anderson and 2nd Lt. Ben Burrows, did a masterful job of bringing our plane to a safe stop, although slipping gently off the end of the runway.

Sgt. Negrette had completed 15 missions when the war in Europe ended in May 1945.

Discharged from the service at Jefferson Barracks, Missouri, Raul returned to Arizona State College at Flagstaff and continued his education under the GI Bill. Receiving a Bachelors degree in 1947, he continued as a graduate student and in 1948 received a Masters degree in education. Over the next 20 years he taught school in Nevada, Arizona and California.

Leaving the teaching profession in 1968, he went into business in Southern California operating a motion picture theater that shows Mexican and other Spanish language films. The business was very successful and at one time he operated as many as four theaters, one being the "Cine Plaza" in Tucson. Raul attributes much of his business success to his wife the former Mary Carol Euzarraga of Phoenix whom he married in 1957. They have one child and reside in California.

Through the years Raul has been an active member of the Vesta Club, Lions, 20-30, American Legion, Knights of Columbus, and Serra International Club. He has served as Vice President of the Spanish Pictures Exhibitors Association. An accomplished musician, Raul played violin for three seasons with the Phoenix Symphony under the direction of Dr. Leslie Hodge.

TECHNICAL SERGEANT RAUL A. NEGRETTE 139

Sgt. Negrette with members of his combat crew. Sgt. Negrette is in the back row, 2nd from left.[1]

---

1. Photo courtesy of Raul A. Negrette.

STAFF SERGEANT MANUEL W. NEVARES

TUCSON

Army Air Corps
Entered Service in July 1942
Flight Engineer/Gunner on medium bombers
13th Attack Squadron, 3rd Attack Group
Pacific Theater, 5th Air Force
Air Medal with OLC

Manny is a graduate of Tucson High School class of 1938. In the summer of 1942, he enlisted in the Air Corps and spent the next nine months training at Sheppard Field, Texas, Will Rogers Field, Oklahoma, and Tyndall Field, Florida, where he completed gunnery school. He was assigned to the Southwest Pacific where he logged 64 combat missions from Hollandia (now Jayapura) and other airfields located on the north coast of New Guinea. As a flight engineer/gunner on B-25 Mitchells, A-20 Havocs and A-26 Invaders, Sgt. Nevares flew bombing and strafing missions against enemy targets. These included Japanese held positions, airdromes, naval vessels and shipping.

Back in Tucson as a civilian, Manny picked up where he left off at Reuben's Arizona Home Supply Company. In 1951 he moved his growing family to California where he was employed in linoleum and carpet laying until his retirement in 1983.

Sgt. Nevares somewhere in the Pacific.[1]

---

1. Photo courtesy of Manuel W. Nevares

STAFF SERGEANT FRANK M. OCHOA

PHOENIX

Army Air Corps
Gunner on B-24
762nd Bomb Squadron, 460th Bomb Group
Mediterranean Theater, 15th Air Force
Air Medal

Sergeant Ochoa, a ball turret gunner, was stationed at Spinazzola Air Field in Italy. On May 10, 1944 he was killed when his Liberator was shot down by flak on a bombing mission to Wiener-Neustadt, Austria.[1] He was on his 6th mission.

---

1. Missing Aircrew Report # 4889, National Archives, Suitland, Maryland

Phoenix Gunner Killed In Action

SGT. FRANK M. OCHOA

Sgt. Frank M. Ochoa, son of Mrs. Dolores M. Bazan, 1139 East Pierce street, has been reported by the International Red Cross as killed in action over Austria, according to word received by Mrs. Bazan from the war department.

Sergeant Ochoa was an aerial gunner.

A requiem high mass will be said at 11 a. m. Sunday at the Immaculate Heart of Mary Church, Ninth and Washington streets.

This article appeared in the Arizona Republic on Sept. 8, 1944.

FLIGHT OFFICER REYES L. OLACHEA

TEMPE

Army Air Corps
Pilot of Waco CG-4A Glider
28th Troop Carrier Squadron, 60th Troop Carrier Group
Mediterranean Theater, 12th Air Force
Air Medal

Reyes completed glider pilot training and received his wings at South Plains Field, Lubbock, Texas, in December, 1943. By spring of the following year he was in Europe preparing for the invasion of southern France. Code-named "Dragoon", this operation began in the early morning hours of August 15, 1944 with the landing of airborne troops by glider and parachute at Le Muy, France. Less than four hours later, three American infantry divisions stormed ashore on the beaches from Cannes to St Tropez.[1] Other campaigns he participated in were in the Balkans and northern Italy.

Returning to the States after the war ended, Reyes remained in the military until his retirement in the early 1960s. He resided in San Jose, California until his death in February, 1991.

---

1. Reader's Digest Illustrated History Of World War II.

Reyes on the left with an unidentified friend[2]

2. Photo courtesy of Charles Olachea

STAFF SERGEANT RUDY L. OLAGUE

ASHFORK/PHOENIX

Army Air Corps
Radio Operator/Gunner on B-17F
322nd Bomb Squadron, 91st Bomb Group
European Theater, 8th Air Force
Air Medal

Sgt. Olague was stationed with the 8th Air Force in Bassingbourn, England. On October 9, 1943, while on a mission over Germany, he was killed when enemy aircraft shot down his Flying Fortress. Sgt. Olague was 19 years old and had flown approximately 7 missions.[1]

---

1. Missing Aircrew Report #0894, National Archives, Suitland, Maryland.

TECHNICAL SERGEANT GREGORIO OLIVA

WINSLOW

Army Air Corps
Radio Operator/Gunner on B-24J
330th Bomb Squadron, 93rd Bomb Group
European Theater, 8th Air Force

On April 8, 1944, Sgt Oliva's B-24 Liberator was shot down over Holland on the return leg of a mission to Brunswick, Germany. He and five members of the ten-man crew survived by bailing out.[1] Sgt. Oliva spent the rest of the war at Stalag XVII B in Austria where another Winslow boy, Sgt. Robert Sanchez (see page 187), was also interned.

---

1. Missing Aircrew Report #3764, National Archives, Suitland, Maryland.

FIRST LIEUTENANT GILBERT DURAN ORRANTIA

CLARKDALE

Army Air Corps
Entered Service November 1941
Pilot on B-25 "Sugar Lump"
446th Bomb Squadron, 321st Bomb Group
Mediterranean Theater, 12th Air Force
Air Medal with 8 OLC

A graduate of Clarkdale High School class of 1936, Gilbert had completed two years at Arizona State College (now Arizona State University) when he volunteered for the Army Air Corps. Accepted as a cadet, he was sent to Arledge Field in Stamford, Texas, for the primary phase of pilot training. There he learned to fly the Stearman PT-17 and the Fairchild PT-19. Moving on to basic flight school at Randolph Field near San Antonio, Texas, known then as the "West Point of the Air", he trained on BT-9s.

Lt. Orrantia with members of his combat crew at Souk El Arba, North Africa. Front row: L to R Chamberlain, McNeil, Kemp. Back row: L to R: Orrantia, Bettinger, Ramirez.

His advanced flight training was at Ellington Field near Houston, Texas, where he flew Cessnas and AT-9s. In August 1942, Gilbert received his pilot wings and gold bars of a second lieutenant. Leaving Texas, he continued to train at Army air fields in South Carolina, Louisiana and Florida, learning the tactics he would use in combat flying the Mitchell B-25.[1]

Arriving in North Africa in November 1942, Gilbert's first missions were in campaigns against Field Marshall Erwin Rommel and the elite troops of his Afrika Korps. Other missions were in support of the invasion of Sicily and tactical targets such as airfields, harbors and bridges

---

1. Built by North American Aviation, the B-25 was a twin engined medium range bomber. The "Mitchell" became a household word on April 18, 1942 when sixteen B-25's were launched from the carrier USS Hornet to bomb Japan. Under the command of Col. James Doolittle, this raid gave Americans a feeling of hope during the early months of the war when Japan was creating havoc in the Pacific. The 1943 best seller "Thirty Seconds over Tokyo", by Captain Ted W. Lawson, gives an account of the Doolittle raid.

on the Italian Peninsula. One of his missions was to Rome to bomb railroad marshalling yards and airfields used by the enemy. He led six aircraft of the 500 planes that participated in the only raid on the Italian capitol. His final missions were flown from Grotaglia, Italy, located about 20 miles north of Taranto. Completing 50 combat missions, (35 as a flight leader), Lt. Orrantia returned to the US in November 1943. Being among the first group of returning pilots with combat experience, he was sent to Greenville, South Carolina, as an instructor in combat tactics.

Lt. Orrantia at Greenville, South Carolina in May 1944.[2]

Discharged from the service in May of 1945, Gilbert returned to Arizona, continued his studies at Arizona State College and graduated in 1947 with a degree in Secondary Education. Unable to find work in his chosen profession, he worked at whatever he could to survive. In 1949 he went to work for the Arizona State Health Department as a Communicable Disease Investigator. His first teaching position was

---

2. All photos courtesy of Gilbert D. Orrantia

with the Mesa, Arizona school system in 1953, where he taught Spanish and French at Mesa High School and later at Westwood High School. Joining the faculty at Mesa Community College in 1967, he taught Spanish and also served as Department Chairman until his retirement in 1983. Professor Orrantia's activities and accomplishments in his professional career and in his civil and personal life are too numerous to mention here. He is listed in Who's Who in American Colleges & Universities in 1947 and Who's Who in Arizona 1984. Gilbert and his wife Sally, a retired educator, have three children.

TECHNICAL SERGEANT ALFONSO M. ORTEGA

PHOENIX

Army Air Corps
Entered Service April 1943
Gunner on B-26 "My Gal Mona"
442nd Bomb Squadron, 320th Bomb Group
Mediterranean Theater, 12th Air Force
Air Medal with 7 OLC, Purple Heart

After completing training at Kearns, Utah and Lowry Field, Colorado, Alfonso was sent to the southeast for pre-combat training on B-17s at Fort Meyers, Florida and Shreveport, Louisiana. In late 1943, he departed Louisiana by plane, bound for the Mediterranean. By this stage of the war, the North African campaign had ended and Axis forces were slowly retreating north on the Italian Peninsula. From airfields in Tunisia, Sardinia, Corsica and France, Sergeant Ortega flew sorties to enemy targets in France, Italy and Germany. He completed 56 missions as a tail-gunner on a Martin B-26 Marauder. On some missions he also served as a "togglier", whose job it was to drop the bombs on command from the lead bombardier's aircraft. On one of his missions he was wounded in the face by flak. On February 15, 1944 he participated in the bombing of the German stronghold at Monte Cassino in Italy. This raid which included B-17s, B-25s and B-26s, dropped over 450 tons of bombs on the Abbey and surrounding area. Although the monastery was totally destroyed, the monks were warned of the impending attack and were able to seek shelter. The results of this mission were not immediately effective, however, for it took an additional three months of heavy fighting by ground troops to dislodge the enemy. Completing his final mission in 1945, Alfonso returned to the US, and was stationed in Santa Ana, California, waiting for reassignment until his discharge in September 1945.[1]

Back in civilian life, he resided in Arizona until 1948 when he moved to Southern California, and was self-employed as a plastering

---

1. Photo courtesy of Alfonso M. Ortega

contractor. Active in his community, he was a volunteer fireman and Fire Chief for the Doheny Fire Department for 35 years. He was a member of the Lions Club of Capistrano for 49 years and participated in taking truckloads of food, clothing, and medical supplies to the poor in Mexico. He also provided eyeglasses to the locals in need. His motto was "Loyalty, Patriotism, Service to my country".

A few months before his death, he had a poignant conversation with his daughter Brenda, over lunch. "What I can't understand is why God spared me while all my buddies were being killed all around me. On one of my missions, a bomb, which had been dropped from one of the planes above, passed through the tail section of my plane. I felt the draft pass my face, I turned to my horror, to see it had gone right through the plane without exploding! Why me? Why did God save me?

He was visibly shaken. Brenda told him God had watched over him because he had a plan for his life. He would build a house and raise a family. In that house, in his living room, the beginnings of the Charismatic Episcopal Church would take shape. That was 1973, and since then over 1000 churches have been established all over the world. At that moment, his eyes opened wide and realized God's plan for his life. "He wept and wept", Brenda writes, "He continues to touch peoples lives even after his death. He was a great man."

Mr. Ortega passed away April 23, 2002 at the age of 77. His wife of 57 years, four children, and thirteen grandchildren survive him.

FIRST LIEUTENANT
JOSE V. ORTEGA

TUCSON

Army Air Corps
Entered Service in July 1941
Bombardier on B-24G Liberator
515th Bomb Squadron, 376th Bomb Group
Mediterranean Theater, 15th Air Force
Air Medal with OLC

Jose was a graduate of Tucson High School class of 1937. While serving with the US Army as an enlisted man, he was accepted as a cadet for bombardier training. After being commissioned a second lieutenant at Big Springs, Texas, and completing pre combat training, Lt. Ortega was assigned overseas to the Mediterranean Theater in March of 1944. He began flying combat missions with the 376th Bomb Group stationed at San Pancrazio, a small town located about 30 miles east of Taranto in southern Italy. On August 17, 1944 while on a mission to bomb the Astra Romana oil refinery at Ploesti in Romania,

Jose was killed when his B-24 Liberator crashed after being hit by flak over the target. Ploesti, a major source of petroleum for the Axis forces, was heavily defended with anti-aircraft batteries. Although there were three crewmembers that survived by bailing out, Jose and five of his fellow airmen were trapped in the burning ship when it went into a spin. Lt. Ortega was 25 years old and had flown approximately 27 prior missions. He is buried at Jefferson Barracks National Cemetery, St. Louis, Missouri. [1] [2]

---

1. Photo courtesy of Gilbert Ortega.
2. Missing Aircrew Report #7980, National Archives, Suitland, Maryland.

SERGEANT
JOE B. PACHECO

PHOENIX

Army Air Corps
Gunner
400th Bomb Squadron, 90th Bomb Group
Pacific Theater, 5th Air Force
Silver Star Posthumously

Will Receive Son's Award

LUKE FIELD, Nov. 26—In the Immaculate Heart of Mary Church, where she and her family have worshipped for many years, Mrs. Mercy L. Pacheco, of 1510 East Washington Street, Phoenix, Sunday will receive the Silver Star, awarded her son, Staff Sgt. Joe B. Macheco, reported missing in action.

The presentation will be made at 11:50 a. m. by Lt. Col. Claude L. Brignall of Luke Field in the presence of parishioners of the Catholic Church. Father Catalina will take part in the ceremonies.

A citation from the headquarters of Lt. Gen. George C. Kenney, commanding general of the Fifth Air Force, said the Silver Star was awarded Sergeant Pachaco "for gallantry in action in Ambon Harbor on Jan. 21, 1943."

Sergeant Pacheca, 23, graduated from Phoenix Union High School in 1938 and completed his aerial gunnery training at Las Vegas, Nev., in May, 1942. He then was sent to Australia.

Two other sons of Mr. and Mrs. Joseph Pacheco are in the service of their country—Sgt. Alex Pacheco, 21, with the army in New Guinea, and John Pacheco, 17, seaman, second class, in the navy.

Their father is a veteran of World War I.

Sgt. Pacheco was a graduate of Phoenix Union High School class of 1938. Sgt. Pacheco was a crewmember on an aircraft that disappeared 50 miles off Hood Point near Brisbane, Australia on February 12, 1943. His plane was on an armed reconnaissance mission. None of the 11 aboard survived.[1] He was awarded the Silver Star posthumously for gallantry in action on a mission to Ambon Harbor in Indonesia. This news item appeared in the Phoenix Gazette on November 26, 1943.

---

1. Missing Aircrew Report #16424, National Archives, Suitland, Maryland.

CORPORAL RICHARD S. PEYRON

TUCSON

Army Air Corps
Gunner on B-24
2nd Bomb Squadron, 22nd Bomb Group
Pacific Theater, 5th Air Force

On June 25, 1945, less than two months before Japan surrendered, CPL Peyron was killed when enemy aircraft shot down his plane. His B-24 Liberator was returning to base from a bombing mission to Makassar on Celebes Island in Indonesia, and crashed in the vicinity of Maros.[1]

---

1. Missing Aircrew Report #14925, National Archives, Suitland, Maryland.

LIEUTENANT ALPHONSE D. QUINONES

MESA

Army Air Corps
Entered service 1939
Pilot of P-38 Lightning
39th Fighter Squadron, 35th Fighter Group
Pacific Theater, 5th Air Force
Air Medal, Purple Heart

In early November 1943, while on a mission to attack the Japanese stronghold at Rabaul, Lt. Quinones was forced to bail out of his stricken P-38. He was on his seventh mission. The Missing Aircrew Report gives the following account.[1]

---

1. Missing Aircrew Report #3037, National Archives, Suitland, Maryland.

THIRTY NINTH FIGHTER SQUADRON
OFFICE OF THE OPERATIONS OFFICER
APO # 713 Unit 2.

Feb.18,1944.

C E R T I F I C A T E

Lieut. Quinones was flying to. 2 position in Red flight, which was leading the formation in combat. On first pass Lieut. Quinones plane was hit in right Engine and he was trailing Prestone badly. Lieut. Flood, who was flying No. 3 position in the flight, stayed with him and started coaching him as to what he should do. Lieut. Quinones followed his instructions. Lieut. Quinones then reported the engine was on fire on both sides. About this time, three Zeros tried to attack from the rear and above, but were driven off by Lieut. Walters and Urquhart who had been following above. Seeing the fire increasing Lieut. Flood told him to release the Canopy. After telling him to bail out Lieut. Flood saw something leave the ship immediately. They were seperated by some distance, but Lieut. Flood is sure that he went straight out of the Cockpit and above the stabalizer. Circling directly over the chute in a vertical bank at approximately 9,000 ft. and 150 M.P.H. Lieut Flood saw a Zero diving on him. After taking evasive action he could not see the Zero or the chute. When last seen, the chute was very close to the ground approx. 200 yards South of Powell River and 3 to 5 miles inland from Wide Bay.

This report is taken from the Combat Report submitted Nov. 7,1943, due to the fact that Lieut. Flood has returned to the States. This report is Certified True and Correct.

JOHN H. LANE
1st Lieut., AAF.
Operations Officer.

LIEUTENANT ALPHONSE D. QUINONES

Missing

Mesa Fighter Pilot

Word was received here Tuesday by Mrs. Grace Quinones that her husband, Lt. Al D. Quinones is missing in action in Europe.

The army officer, a P-38 fighter pilot, has been in the service since 1939 and was in Hawaii during the bombing of Pearl Harbor. He received his advanced training at Williams Field.

Mrs. Quinones and his mother, Mrs. Elsie Quinones are living at 232 South Morris street.

Rabaul, located on the north Coast of New Britain Island in the Bismarck Archipelago was about 500 miles from Lt. Quinones's base at Port Moresby on the island of New Guinea. After bailing out of his burning aircraft, Lt. Quinones wandered in the jungle for seven days before being turned over to the Japanese by the island natives. He would spend the next twenty-three months in Rabaul as a POW. In his book *M.I.A. Over Rabaul*, fellow internee John B. Kepchia describes the intolerable conditions the prisoners experienced.

The news item on the left appeared in the Mesa Journal Tribune on November 18, 1943. It states in error that he was in Europe.

> **Mesa Lions Honor World War Dead**
>
> MESA, May 10—Sixteen soldier dead of the present World War were posthumously awarded citations by the City of Mesa through the Mesa Lions Club at a meeting held Wednesday in El Portal Hotel. J. S. Jarvis, Ronald Ellsworth and J. C. Anderson served as chairman of the meeting and the committee in charge of citations.
>
> The soldier dead whose parents or other relatives represented them at the meeting, are Walter Scott, James Ruiz, Robert Ryan, Warren Montgomery, Bill McCary, Lemuel Miguel, Quinton Martin, John Stradling, Orlando Loera, Alvin Inglish, Robert S. Johnson, Sam Brown, Norman Stapley, Clarence Stapp, Al D. Quinones, and Marshall Stewart.
>
> Eighty persons were present at the citations meeting during which each family represented was present a scroll with the citation inscribed in black against a background of gold.

Unlike the German POW camps in Europe, POWs at Rabaul did not have contact with the International Red Cross. Therefore, there was no official US government list that gave the names of those interned there.

Several months after his capture, Lt. Quinones's status was changed by the War Department from Missing in Action (MIA) to Finding of Death (FOD) and his family in Mesa were notified. In the spring of 1944 his family attended a ceremony honoring those that had died in the war. The news item above appeared in the Phoenix Gazette on May 10, 1944.

As was happening all across the USA, the death of someone serving in the military was a tragic family experience. It was especially difficult for those families where the body of their loved one was not recovered for burial overseas or at home. Even though Lt. Quinones was listed as dead by the government, his family refused to give up hope. Since there was no certainty of his death, perhaps he might still be alive in a POW camp or evading capture by hiding out in some remote island jungle. They would not learn he was alive until after the war ended in September of 1945.

Mesa Officer Is Liberated

LEYTE, Philippines, Oct. 4—(AP)—Six American airmen, imprisoned by Japanese on Rabaul, huddled gleefully in a bomb shelter and for 24 hours listened happily to the aerial obliteration of Rabaul's famed Chinatown—and the killing of many of their Nipponese captors.

Lt. Jose Holguin, Los Angeles, described the smashing American air raids of March, 1944, which left "dead Japs everywhere." The intensive bombing lasted 51 consecutive days, he said.

Rescued and brought to the Philippines with Holguin were Lts. (jg) Joseph Gates Nason, West Boro, Mass.; Alfonse Quinones, 232½ South Morris Street, Mesa, Ariz.; and James A. McMurria, Columbus, Ga.; S/Sgt. Escoe E. Palmer, Gainsville, Ga.; and Aviation Radioman 2/c John B. Kepchia, Greensburg, Pa.

In the closing days of the war, they said, the Japanese major commanding their prison camp doled out two moldy cigarets to each prisoner and began talking of his plans to give them more freedom. They knew then that the war had ended, Holguin said.

"In the last few months even the guards seemed to know they were licked and began doing us small favors," he added.

The news item on the left appeared in the Phoenix Gazette on October 4, 1945. Lt. Quinones was one of six Americans and one Australian who survived out of seventy interned at Rabaul during the war. These figures equate to a 90 percent death rate and show Rabaul may have been one of the worst run POW camps of WWII.[2]

---

2. In his book *Ghost Soldiers,* Hampton Sides states on page 23 that "after the war, it would be calculated that the death rate of Allied POWs held in German and Italian camps was approximately 4 percent. In Japanese-run camps, the death rate was 27 percent."

Lt. Al Quinones with members of his squadron at Port Moresby, New Guinea, 1943. Al is in the front row, 2nd from left[3]

3. Photo courtesy of Al Quinones

Enroute to a hospital in the Philippines after being liberated are L to R:
James MacMurria, Al Quinones, Joe Holguin, Escoe Palmer, and John Kepchia.[4]

Returning home, Al spent a year recuperating at a hospital in Santa Fe, New Mexico. He remained in the military and was stationed at Luke AFB in Arizona during the Korean War. In other duties he served as the interpreter for the Air Force Thunderbirds on their first international tour through Latin America. In 1955, he was assigned to the Dominican Republic as the Defense Attache and later to Dow AFB in Bangor, Maine. In July 1960, he retired with twenty-two years of service and the rank of major. He returned to Arizona and attended Arizona State University where he received several degrees in preparation for a teaching career. He taught Spanish and science at St. Mary's High School in Phoenix. He also taught in eastern Arizona at Round Valley High School in Eager and St. John's High School. Upon leaving the

---

4. Photo courtesy of John B. Kepchia

teaching profession, he returned to Mesa where he resided until his death in May 2002. His wife, four children and eight grandchildren survive him[5]

---

5. Note: After reading the November 18, 1943 news item where Al Quinones was listed as MIA, I began research to determine if he had survived the war. My question was quickly answered when I saw the FOD (Finding Of Death) next to his name in *The Honor List of Dead and Missing for the State of Arizona*. Assuming he was dead based on this fact, I reduced my research activity on him until I came across the October 4, 1945 news item that he had been liberated. With this, my research activity resumed, and I set out to locate Al or his survivors. I was unsuccessful in my early attempts to find him until I was able to contact his fellow internee and good friend, Jose Holguin, who gave me Al's address. Contacting Al, I learned that he was not from Arizona, but had come here during the war to complete his pilot training at Williams Field, where he won his wings. Moving with him to Arizona at that time was his wife Grace whom he had married while stationed in Texas. Also moving to Mesa about this time was his mother and Al's younger siblings.

   Al was born in Mayaguez, Puerto Rico and brought as a baby to New York City by his parents. He graduated with honors from Stuyvesant High School in New York and was with the Civilian Conservation Corps (CCC) in Nevada prior to joining the Army in the fall of 1939.

STAFF SERGEANT MANUEL A. RAMIREZ

PHOENIX

Army Air Corps
Gunner on B-24H
732nd Bomb Squadron, 453rd Bomb Group
European Theater, 8th Air Force
Air Medal

On May 8, 1944, Sgt. Ramirez was killed when enemy aircraft shot down his Liberator. Flying as ball turret gunner, he was on a mission to Brunswick, Germany, from his base in Old Buckenham, England. [1]

---

1. Missing Aircrew Report #4596, National Archives, Suitland, Maryland

STAFF SERGEANT MANUEL M. RAMOS

DOUGLAS

Army Air Corps
Radio Operator/Gunner on B-17G
544th Bomb Squadron, 384th Bomb Group
European Theater, 8th Air Force

On May 24, 1944, Sgt. Ramos's Flying Fortress took a direct hit of flak in the number 2 engine while on a mission to Berlin. Nine crewmembers including Ramos bailed out. He was wounded by a German fighter while descending in his chute and died later in a German hospital. One other crewmember died and seven were captured. This occurred about 40 miles north of Berlin near the village of Hertzberg. [1]

---

1. Missing Aircrew Report #5268, National Archives, Suitland, Maryland.

SERGEANT MIGUEL A. REYES

TUCSON

Army Air Corps
Entered Service March 1943
Gunner on B-24J
856th Bomb Squadron, 492nd Bomb Group
European Theater, 8th Air Force

On June 20, 1944, Sgt. Reyes, the right waist gunner, was killed when his B-24 Liberator was shot down by enemy aircraft. He was on a mission to Politz, Germany from his base in North Pickenham, England. This was his fourth mission.[1]

---

1. Missing Aircrew Report #7084, National Archives, Suitland, Maryland.

AMM2
EVERARDO R. REYNOSO

RAY/SONORA

US Navy
Entered Service May 1943
Flight Engineer/Gunner on PBM-3
Air Rescue Squadron 3 (VH-3)
Pacific Theater
Air Medal

Immediately upon graduating from Ray High School in May 1943, Everardo volunteered for the air service branch of the Navy. He completed basic training in San Diego, California, basic flight training at Lake City Naval Air Station (NAS) in Florida, and advanced training at Alameda NAS in California. During this period he trained on the Beech SNB, Lockheed PV-1, PV-2, and Martin PBM-3. In early 1944 he received his flight engineers wings at Alameda, and was soon assigned to VH-3, an air rescue squadron operating in the South Pacific Theater. Flying PBM-3 Mariners, often called "Dumbos," the duties of this squadron were to patrol for enemy submarines and perform air-sea rescue of pilots and crew members who had ditched at sea. In the waters around Okinawa during the spring of 1945, his crew made 10 open sea landings to pick up 12 American fighting men adrift. On one day in late April near the island of Kikai in the Ryukyus chain south of Japan, they made three open sea landings in rough waters while under heavy enemy fire from shore. Rescued were an Army Air Corps captain flying a Republic P-47, a Marine second lieutenant flying a Chance Vought F4U, and a Navy lieutenant flying a Grumman F6F. While operating in the forward combat areas, Everardo's aircraft and crew were serviced and re-supplied by the USS Bearing Strait (AVP34), an aircraft tender.

When the war ended, the 21-year-old Aviation Machinist Mate Second Class remained in the Navy and was stationed at Guam until his return to the States in December 1947. Back in civilian life, Everardo held civil service positions with the Navy and Air Force. He was also a member of the Air Force Reserve, and in 1981 participated in the rescue of nine people from the fire of the MGM hotel in Las Vegas. He is married to the former Rose Soto of Glendale. Arizona. They have four children, eleven grandchildren, and seven great-grandchildren. They reside in Glendale.

STAFF SERGEANT JOE P. RUIZ

PHOENIX

Army Air Corps
Entered Service 1942

The following news item appeared in the Arizona Republic on April 15, 1944.

Sergeant Dies In Plane Crash

STAFF SGT. JOE RUIZ

Staff Sgt. Joe P. Ruiz, jr., 20-year-old son of Mr. and Mrs. Joe P. Ruiz, 15 East Hadley street, was reported killed in an airplane accident in Tunisia March 11, according to word received by his parents from the war department yesterday.

Sergeant Ruiz, a bombardier on a Flying Fortress, was a former employee of the circulation department of the Republic and Gazette. He entered the service January 5, 1942 and had been overseas only about a month prior to his death.

He attended Phoenix Union High School. His last letter home was written on March 10, the day before the fatal crash.

SERGEANT JESUS M. SALAS

GLOBE

Army Air Corps
Gunner on B17G
367th Bomb Squadron, 306th Bomb Group
European Theater, 8th Air Force

Sgt. Salas was the ball turret gunner on a B-17 Flying Fortress. On May 8, 1944 while on a mission to Berlin, he was killed when his plane collided with two other B-17s near Perleberg, Germany.[1] Sgt. Salas was a graduate of Globe High School class of 1938.

---

1. Missing Aircrew Report #4554, National Archives, Suitland, Maryland.

STAFF SERGEANT ALBERT M. SALAZAR

PHOENIX

Army Air Corps
Gunner on B-17G
327th Bomb Squadron, 92nd Bomb Group
European Theater, 8th Air Force

On October 7, 1944, Sgt. Salazar, the ball turret gunner on a Flying Fortress, was killed in action. His plane was shot down by enemy flak while on a mission to Zwickau, Germany, from his base in Podington, England. Site of the crash was north of Dresden.[1]

---

1. Missing Aircrew Report #9345, National Archives, Suitland, Maryland.

TECHNICAL SERGEANT ROBERT L. SANCHEZ

WINSLOW

Army Air Corps
Entered Service July 1942
Radio Operator/Gunner on B-17F
364th Bomb Squadron, 305th Bomb Group
European Theater, 8th Air Force
Air Medal, Purple Heart

Robert is a graduate of Winslow High School class of 1941. Entering the service in the summer of 1942, he was in training for approximately one year at army airfields in Illinois and Texas. His pre-combat training was with the "Colonel Savoi Group", the first forty crews of the 305th Bomb Group. In the summer of 1943, he flew with this group bound for Chelveston, England via Newfoundland, Scotland and Ireland.

As the ball turret gunner on a B-17, he began flying missions to bomb German targets across the English Channel. One of these was an unsuccessful attempt to find the German battleship Scharn Horst that was reported to be at Gdynia, Poland on the Baltic Sea coast.

On October 14, 1943, Robert's Flying Fortress was shot down by enemy aircraft over Holland, enroute to bomb the ball bearing factories in Schweinfurt, Germany. Nine of the ten crewmembers were able to escape the doomed plane by parachute. Only Lieutenant Boggs, the copilot, did not bail out. Sgt. Sanchez was on his 9th mission.[1]

This mission to Schweinfurt, deep into Germany, is infamous in the history of the Army Air Corps because of heavy losses suffered. It is known as "Second Schweinfurt" to distinguish it from the first mission to Schweinfurt on August 17, 1943, also with heavy losses. Robert recommends the book "Wrong Place! Wrong Time!" by George C. Kuhl, which details the events of that fateful day.

Taken prisoner, Sgt. Sanchez was sent to Stalag XVII B in Austria where he spent the next 18 months. His hometown was well represented when Sgt. Gregorio Olivas, also from Winslow, ended up at the same POW camp after his plane was shot down in May, 1944.

Returning to civilian life, Robert worked for the US Postal Service in Winslow for thirty years until a heart attack forced him to retire. He was married to the former Virginia Chavez of Winslow. They have ten children.

---

1. Missing Aircrew Report #0912, National Archives, Suitland, Maryland.

Robert Sanchez with fellow crewmembers during training in July 1943.[2]
Front row L to R: Norris, Spadafora, Smith, Sanchez, Knapp, Wilson
Back row L to R: Eakle, Collins, Boggs, Anderson

---

2. Photo courtesy of Robert L. Sanchez

FIRST LIEUTENANT HECTOR J. SANTA ANNA

MIAMI

Army Air Corps
Entered Service July 1942
Pilot on B-17G "Bachelors Delight"
832nd Bomb Squadron, 486th Bomb Group
European Theater, 8th Air Force
Air Medal with 6 OLC

Hector is a graduate of Miami High School class of 1940. Accepted as an aviation cadet in the summer of 1942, he began a yearlong period of pilot training at various army airfields in Texas.

Preflight school was at Kelly Field, Texas where he learned the rudiments of flight theory as well as the customs and traditions of military life. His first introduction to actual flying was during primary flight school at Corsicana, Texas. There he trained on the PT-19, and after logging twelve and a half hours of flight time, completed his first solo flight. The next phase, basic flight school, was at Majors Field near Greenville, Texas, where he trained on the Vultee BT-13. The final phase, advanced flight school, was at Brooks Field at San Antonio, Texas where he flew the AT-6 Texan. There, in July 1943, he received his silver pilot wings and the gold bars of second lieutenant.

Selected for flight instructor training, Lt. Santa Anna was sent to school at Randolph Field, Texas, the "West Point of the Air." Upon completion he was assigned as a flight instructor for Central and South American military officers and cadets attending basic flight training at Waco Army Air Field, Texas. Volunteering for combat duty in August 1944, he was sent to Alexandria, Louisiana, for B-17 combat crew training. There he learned the necessary skills together with the crewmembers that would accompany him into combat.

Assigned to the European Theater, he and his crew arrived in England in late October 1944 after having flown a new B-17G from Lincoln, Nebraska, to Valley, Wales via Gander, Newfoundland and Rekjavic, Iceland. He and his crew were assigned to the 486th Bomb Group, 3rd Bomb Wing, of the 8th Air Force, stationed at Sudbury, Suffolk County, about 50 miles NE of London.

From November 16, 1944 to March 3, 1945, Lt. Santa Anna flew as aircraft commander on 34 (plus one as observer) combat missions to targets in Germany. His radio operator, Sergeant Harry G. Johnson from Joplin, Missouri, kept a diary where he recorded certain data and events for each mission. Two missions, numbers 9 and 31, are printed here from this diary.

> *Mission # 9 December 24, 1944*
> *Airfield at Aschaffenburg, Germany*
> *Ship # 937*
> *Bomb Load 14-250 lbs.*
> *4-500 lbs. Incendiaries*
> *Bomb Altitude 22,000 feet*
> *Heavy Flak*
> *Briefing Officer told us that today saw the greatest air fleet ever assembled. 8th Air Force put up 2000 heavy bombers, besides P-51s, P-47s and B-26s from 9th Air Force. Perfect day for bombing. Never saw so many airplanes in my life.*
> *Beautiful sight to see all the formations. Lost #2 engine by an old leak. Lucky it didn't catch fire. Length of mission-seven and a half hours. We sure gave a damn good Christmas today to the "Jerrys."*

Mission #31 February 25, 1945
Rail yards at Munich, Germany
Ship # 027 (Bachelors Delight)
Bomb load 6-1000 lbs
Very very heavy flak
Over 100 holes in ship, roughest one yet.
How we all got out without a scratch, I'll never know. The ship looked like a sieve. Flak got #2 engine and shot it out. Got right side oxygen system, both tires, #3 oil tank, cylinders in #4 engine, elevator controls, #3 supercharger, both outside and wing tanks.
I never prayed so hard or was more scared in my life. I thought that this was "it". Santa Anna made a beautiful crash landing with both tires flat, in Brussels, Belgium. They told us our ship was beyond repair and would be salvaged. Flak suits saved 3 of the guys. What kept us from catching fire, I'll never know; #2 (engine) leaked oil all over the wings, fuselodge, fin and stablizer. Lucky outside gas tanks didn't catch fire. Had a gay time in Brussels. Women, champagne, beer and cognac. Pretty shaky after the mission, but the alcohol pulled us through. Flew back the next day with RAF (Royal Air Force) in a C-47, we all got back. Santa Anna finally made 1st Lieutenant on his birthday the 26th. God grant us luck to finish up soon and all in one piece. Put Lou's name on all the bombs. Length of Mission-8hrs.

194   Arizona's Hispanic Flyboys 1941-1945

Hector with his combat crew at Alexandria, Louisiana
in September 1944.[1]
Front row L to R: H. Santa Anna, J. Chenoweth, K. Christoph,
C. Seibel
Back row L to R: H. Martin, H. Johnson, C. Chandler, W. Cross, W.
Johnson. V. Hilt

Completing his final combat mission in March 1945, Hector was assigned to the Air Transport Command (ATC later to be known as the Military Air Transport Service) at Love Field (Dallas), Texas where he flew various types of aircraft. By the end of 1945, he had undergone flight training in transports, and began flying transport missions worldwide from his new post at Westover AFB, Massachusetts. Lt. Santa Anna continued flying as aircraft commander and flight instructor in C-54s, C-97s and C-121s with the ATC. From August 1948 to January 1949 he flew 127 missions into Templehof Aerodrome in one of the important early events of the cold war, the Berlin Airlift. Transferring to the Strategic Air Command (SAC) in 1951, he completed

---

1.   Photo courtesy of Hector J. Santa Anna

training on the B-36 bomber. He was then selected to be command pilot for the SAC's first flying command post-a C-97 equipped with sophisticated radar and radio gear.

In the years that followed, Hector saw service with the Joint U.S. Military Group (JUSMG) in Madrid, Spain; the Air Force Systems Command, Andrews AFB, MD; and the Office of Secretary of Defense (Public Affairs). While assigned to the Pentagon in Washington D.C., he continued his education at the University of Maryland obtaining a BS, cum laude, in public administration in 1962. In June 1964, with 22 years of service, he retired with the rank of lieutenant colonel. His decorations include the Air Medal with 6 OLC, Air Force Commendation Medal, Army Commendation Medal, Joint Service Commendation Medal, WWII Victory Medal, Humane Action Medal (Berlin Airlift), National Defense Service Medal, United States Service Medal, American Campaign Medal, and the Army of Occupation Medal (Germany). Later that same year he accepted a position with civil service, and for the next 19 years held various administrative and management assignments with the Navy, NASA, OEO, and FAA.

After his retirement from government, he remained active in aviation by teaching evening classes at Catonsville Community College, and as chief flight instructor with the US Naval Academy Flying Club.

There is not sufficient space here to adequately document the experiences and accomplishments of Mr. Santa Anna. During his almost 50 years as an aviator in service of his country, he logged nearly 12,000 hours of flight time and 3900 hours of flight instruction, and is the recipient of numerous honors and awards.

Hector is married to the former Olive Allen of Lubbock, Texas. They have two children and five grandchildren.

SERGEANT
FRED C. SAUCEDO

GILA COUNTY (Home Town Unknown)

Army Air Corps
Gunner on B-17G
511th Bomb Squadron, 351st Bomb Group
European Theater, 8th Air Force

On March 18, 1944 while on his first mission, Sgt. Saucedo, the tail gunner on a B-17 Flying Fortress, was killed along with most members of the crew. They were on the return trip after having bombed Augsburg in southern Germany, when their formation was attacked head on by ME109s.[1]

---

1. Missing Aircrew Report #3236, National Archives, Suitland, Maryland.

FIRST LIEUTENANT MIGUEL M. SERNA

RAY/SONORA

Army Air Corps
Entered Service July 1942
Bombardier on B-24 "Ben's Folly"
576th Bomb Squadron, 392nd Bomb Group
European Theater, 8th Air Force
Distinguished Flying Cross, Air Medal with 6 OLC

Upon graduating from Ray High School in the spring of 1942, Mike joined the Air Corps and was accepted as a cadet for bombardier training. During the next 16 months he was in various phases of training at army airfields located in Texas, Colorado and New Mexico. He received his silver wings and commission as a second lieutenant in Midland, Texas, in October 1943. Following a period of pre-combat training at Colorado Springs, Colorado, the 19 year old junior officer departed Wichita, Kansas, on a B-24 Liberator bound for Europe. Assigned to the 392nd bomb group with the 8th Air Force stationed near Thedford, England, Lt. Serna flew his first combat mission on June 15, 1944. This was in support of Allied invasion forces that had landed on the Normandy coast June 6 (D-Day). Other missions followed to various targets located in Germany, France, and Holland. Some of those which stand out in his memory after more than 50 years were the raid on the oil refineries at Politz on June 20th, and two missions to Munich on July 11th and 12th. These long haul flights, deep into Germany, were heavily defended by enemy fighter aircraft and anti-aircraft batteries. His 26th mission was a low-level supply drop to Holland, where the German soldiers could be seen firing their rifles from rooftops.

Following his next mission on September 29, 1944, he was commended for a good job when he flew as lead bombardier, using a combination of radar and visual sightings to hit the railroad marshalling yards at Hamm, Germany. Completing his 30th and final mission in December 1944, Lt. Serna returned to the US and was stationed at various bases as an instructor until the war ended. With the reduction in forces after the war, Mike remained in the Air Corps (name changed to Air Force in 1947) as a non-commissioned officer. From July to November 1951 during the Korean War, he flew 60 combat missions with a B-26 night intruder group stationed at Yokosuka, Japan. Taking advantage of the Air Force's operation "Bootstrap" educational program, he obtained a Bachelors degree in 1956 from Omaha University and a Masters degree in 1960 from the University of Colorado. While serving as chief master sergeant at Colorado Springs in 1962, he was recalled to active duty in his commissioned rank of major. In October 1968 with 26 years of service and the rank of lieutenant colonel, he retired from the Air Force. In addition to those mentioned above, his decorations include the Air Force Commendation Medal, Good Conduct Medal, WWII Victory Medal, Army of Occupation Medal, and Theater of Operation ribbons (ETO and Korea) Joining the faculty of Northern State College at Aberdeen, South Dakota, Professor Serna taught management and finance courses until his retirement in 1987.

Mike is married to the former Anita Schaunaman of Aberdeen, South Dakota. They have two children, and seven grandchildren.

Mike Serna with members of his combat crew in Colorado Springs.[1]
Front row L to R: Daniels, Holliday, McCutheon, Serna.
Back row L to R: Johnson, Rambo, Wattles, Sevier, Negus, Phillips.

---

1. All photos courtesy of Mike Serna

LIEUTENANT ROBERT S. SOSA

DOUGLAS

Army Air Corps
Entered Service February 1943
Navigator on B-24H
564th Bomb Squadron, 389th Bomb Group
European Theater, 8th Air Force

Lt. Sosa was a graduate of Arizona State College in Tempe class of 1942. On April 29, 1944, while on a mission to Berlin, Germany, Lt. Sosa was killed when his B-24 Liberator was shot down by enemy aircraft.[1]

---

1. Missing Aircrew Report #4494, National Archives, Suitland, Maryland

STAFF SERGEANT CHARLES M. SOTELO

BISBEE

Army Air Corps
Entered Service January 1943
Gunner on B-24
Pacific Theater, 5th Air Force
Air Medal, Purple Heart

Charles received his training in aviation mechanics at Sheppard Field, near Wichita Falls, Texas, and in aerial gunnery at Tyndall Field, near Panama City, Florida. On May 27, 1944, Sgt. Sotelo, a veteran of 50 missions, was killed when his B-24 Liberator was shot down in New Guinea.

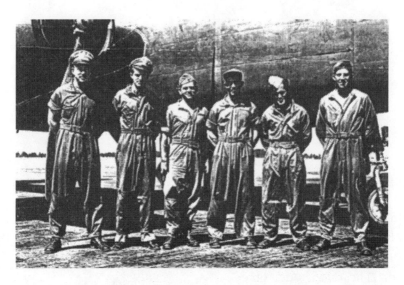

Sgt. Sotelo, 2nd from right, and some members of his aircrew[1]

---

1. Photo courtesy of Manuel M. Sotelo

CAPTAIN
OSCAR C. SOTO

NOGALES

Army Air Corps
Entered Service August 12, 1940
Pilot
6th Ferrying Group, 556th AAF Base Unit
Pacific Theater, China-Burma-India Theater

Oscar is a graduate of Nogales High School class of 1940. Enlisting in the Air Corps in August of that year, he was assigned to Lowry Field, Denver, Colorado, and later to Scott Field, Illinois, where he completed radio operator school. When Pearl Harbor was attacked in December 1941, Oscar was stationed at Lowry Field, where he was flying as radio operator on a B-18 bomber. Accepted as a cadet for pilot training, he was sent to Douglas, Georgia, for preflight and primary flight training, where he soloed on the Stearman PT-17 after fewer than nine hours of instruction. The next phase, basic flight school, was at Maxwell Field in Montgomery, Alabama, where he flew the Vultee BT-13. The final phase, advanced flight school, was at Napier Field in Dothan, Alabama, where he trained on the AT-6 Texan, and in June 1943 received his silver pilot wings and gold bars of a second lieutenant. Continuing his training at Pennsylvania Central Airlines in Roanoke, Virginia, he was certified (checked out) to fly Douglas DC-3s. Five months later, he was assigned to the 6th Ferrying Group in Long Beach, California. Checked out on B-24s, B-17s, A-20s, P-38s, C-47s and B-25s, he began delivering these aircraft to air bases in the United States and Australia. After a two month training period on C-46 Curtis Commandos in Reno, Nevada, he began flying this transport from Miami, Florida, to Spanish Morocco in North Africa. He also flew a "Milk Run" from Casa Blanca to Cairo to Karachi, India.

In 1945 he volunteered to fly the "Hump" over the Himalayan Mountains into China. On this run he completed thirty missions, transporting cargo such as gasoline, soldiers, and gold bullion from Mohamberi Burma to Kung Ming, China.

Discharged from the service in March 1946, Oscar returned to Nogales. Obtaining his flight instructor's certificate and examiner's certificate he began giving flight instruction to local Nogales boys who qualified under the GI Bill. In 1950 he was hired as an executive pilot for a prominent produce grower from Sinaloa, Mexico. Returning to Nogales nine years later, he managed and operated his own business until his retirement in 1983. Oscar is married to the former Irma Carrasco of Nogales, Arizona. They have two children and nine grandchildren.[1]

---

1. Photo courtesy of Oscar C. Soto

FIRST LIEUTENANT MANUEL J. TREVINO JR.

SUPERIOR

Army Air Corps
Entered Service June 1942
Pilot on B-24 "Yankee Doodle" and "Bad Penny"
319th Bomb Squadron, 90th Bomb Group, "Jolly Rogers"
Pacific Theater, 5th Air Force
Air Medal with 3 OLC

Within a month after graduating from Superior High School in May 1942, Manuel entered the Army Air Corps. Accepted as a cadet for pilot training, he was sent to Kelly Field in San Antonio, Texas, where he completed preflight school. His primary flight school was at Brayton Field in Cuero, Texas, where he learned to fly the PT-19 and completed his first solo flight after seven hours of hands-on instruction. The next phase, basic flight school was at Perrin Field in Sherman, Texas, where he trained on the Vultee BT-13. For advanced flight school he was sent to Lubbock, Texas, for training on the Cessna AT-17. It was there in April 1943, just one month after his 19th birthday, that he received his pilot wings. He was the youngest graduate in his class of 234 students. Being an enlisted man and also due to his age, he was given the rank of Flight Officer which was a non-commissioned rank similar to a Warrant Officer in today's military.

Selected for bombers, Manuel returned to his home state for training on B-24 Liberators at Davis-Monthan Field in Tucson. While there he was made aircraft commander, which was quite an accomplishment for someone just one year out of high school. One thrilling moment he reported was when he buzzed his hometown of Superior while on a training flight near this copper mining town north of Tucson. After further training at Pueblo, Colorado, he and his crew picked up a new B-24 in Topeka, Kansas, and flew to Fairfield, California, where they departed for the Pacific Theater in the late summer of 1943.

Assigned to the 319th Bomb Squadron of the 90th Bomb Group stationed at Port Moresby, New Guinea, Flight Officer Trevino was, at 19, the youngest aircraft commander in the "Jolly Rogers." Because of their youth, he and his crew were known as the "high school bunch" within the squadron.

Promoted to second lieutenant soon after his 20th birthday, Manuel continued flying combat missions to bomb Japanese targets throughout the vast southwest Pacific area of the 5th Air Force. By November, 1944, he had completed 66 missions. One of these was an 18-hour round trip flight from his base on Biak Island to hit the oil refineries at Balikpapan in Borneo.

During his combat tour in the Pacific, Manuel was recommended for the Distinguished Flying Cross, but it was denied because, as he was told, "General Kenney says we have too many heroes and the war is almost over."

After finishing his combat tour, Lt. Trevino returned to Texas where he completed the instrument school for instructors at Bryon in March 1945. Obtaining his commercial pilot's license, he was recruited by American Airlines prior to his release from the service. Discharged in July, 1945, he was unable to accept the airline's offer, instead, taking over the family business after his father became seriously ill.

Founded in 1944 by his father, Manuel Sr., Oxnard Music Systems was located in Oxnard, California. Over a 32-year period, Manuel Jr. expanded and successfully operated the business until his retirement in 1977. He is married to the former Jessie Flores of Oxnard, and they have four children and 11 grandchildren.

Lt. Trevino and his combat crew in early 1944.[1]
Back Row L to R: J. Enfea, R. Snodgrass, R. Rero, B. Camp, M. Gupot, G. Riess
Front Row L to R: J. Gruenwald, R. White, G. Dacardo, M. Trevino

---

1. Photo courtesy of Manuel J. Trevino

TECHNICAL SERGEANT JOHN R. TRUJILLO

RAY/SONORA

Army Air Corps
Entered Service November 1941
Flight Engineer/Gunner on B-24
737th Bomb Squadron, 545th Bomb Group
Mediterranean Theater, 15th Air Force
Air Medal

Upon entering the Air Corps, John was sent to Wichita Falls, Texas, and Pueblo, Colorado, for aircraft mechanics training. He then spent about six weeks at Boeing Aircraft Company in Seattle, Washington, becoming familiar with the B-17 Flying Fortress. Expecting to be assigned permanently to B-17s, he was sent instead to Davis Monthon Field in Tucson for flight engineer training on the B-24 Liberator. From there he went to Charleston, South Carolina, for training with the crew he would fly with in combat. Assigned to the Mediterranean Theater, he arrived in Cerignola, Italy, in early 1944. From this base in southeastern Italy, he flew his first mission in support of the Allied beach landing at Anzio. Other missions he flew were to the Ploesti oil fields in Romania, to southern France, to Germany, and to the German stronghold at Monte Cassino in Italy.

While on a mission to Toulon on the south coast of France in June 1944, his Liberator was hit by enemy fire and was forced to land in

Barcelona, Spain. In the summer of 1944 there was probably no better place in Europe to be "Missing in Action" than Spain. Being fluent in the language also helped, and John and his crew wasted no time in making the best of this "unfortunate situation." Because Spain was a neutral country during the war, there was no fighting going on within its borders and it was relatively safe for downed airmen. However, they did not have complete freedom and there were some restrictions with which they had to comply.

All good times must eventually end, and after about a month they received orders to return to their base in Italy. They left Spain through Gibraltar and crossed the Mediterranean by ship to the city of Algiers in North Africa. From there they returned by plane to Cerignola, where they completed two more missions before the entire crew was shipped back to the US in late 1944.

Sgt. Trujillo with some of his fellow crewmembers in Italy in 1944. John is standing 2nd from left.[1]

---

1. Photo courtesy of John R. Trujillo

After enjoying a little "R & R" in Santa Monica, California, Sergeant Trujillo was stationed at Rantoul, Illinois, and Roswell, New Mexico, until the end of the war. Realizing that employment would be hard to find with all the discharged servicemen entering the job market, John decided to remain in the Air Corps for an additional 18 months. His last tour of duty was spent in Guam until his discharge in April of 1947.

John was called back into the service during the Korean War and was stationed at Nellis Air Force Base in Nevada until his discharge.

Back in civilian life, John worked for Sears in Las Vegas for a few years before moving to San Diego, California, in 1962. There he was employed in the construction field until his retirement in 1980. John is married, and he and his wife reside in Arizona.

CAPTAIN
ROGER E. VARGAS

MORENCI

Army Air Corps
Entered Service in July 1940
Navigator on B-17E and F "Lulu Belle"
63rd Bomb Squadron, 43rd Bomb Group
Pacific Theater, 5th Air Force
Silver Star, Distinguished Flying Cross, Air Medal with 2 OLC, Purple Heart

---

After graduating from Morenci High School in the class of 1935, Roger enrolled at Arizona State College in Flagstaff (now Northern Arizona University). While in college he was active in sports, winning letters in track, cross country and boxing. He graduated with a BA degree in 1939. Entering the Army Air Corps, he was commissioned a 2nd lieutenant upon completing Navigator training in April of 1941 at Pan-American Airways, University of Miami, Coral Gables, Florida.

For his first assignment he served in the Panama Canal Zone from April 1941 to June 1942, flying B-18A and B-17B aircraft on submarine patrol. In August 1942, eight months after America's entry into WWII, Roger arrived in Australia and began flying combat missions with the 19th Bomb Group. Later he joined the 63rd Bomb Squadron of the 43rd Bomb Group, which was newly formed under General George C. Kenney. From bases in Australia and New Guinea, he continued flying missions to enemy targets throughout the Southwest Pacific area of the 5th Air Force. In early March 1943, he participated in the "Battle of the Bismarck Sea" off the north coast of New Guinea. In this famous three-day battle, Allied air forces were successful in destroying a complete Japanese convoy of destroyers and troop transports. For his action during this battle he was later presented the Silver Star. An account of the battle, in which Roger and the crew of the "Lulu Belle" are mentioned, can be found in the book *Flying Buccaneers*, by Steve Birdsall.

Roger and crewmembers in New Guinea, February 1943.
Back Row L to R: E. Johnson, M. Wolverton, C. Hunter, M. Scoggins, P. Bosso. Front Row L to R: F. Denault, C. Anderson, R. Vargas, H. Iverson [1]

In April 1943, while on his 44th combat mission, Roger was wounded while skip-bombing Bogia harbor near Wewak on the north coast of New Guinea. After being hospitalized in Port Moresby for six weeks, he returned to the US. Because of his injuries, he remained grounded until October 1943, when he was assigned as squadron navigator to train combat crews in Walla Walla, Washington, and later in Avon Park, Florida. His next assignment in August, 1944, was as navigator, delivering aircraft worldwide with the 6th Ferrying Group stationed at Long Beach, California. He was flying with this unit delivering B-24s to Australia when the war ended one year later.

After the Japanese surrender, Roger remained in the Air Corps as a crew navigator until October 1950, when he was relieved from flying duties due to a physical disability from his war injury. During his remaining years in the Air Force, while progressing to the rank of lieutenant colonel, he held various management positions in the supply and logistics field. In October 1962, he retired after 22 years of service. His decorations, in addition to those mentioned above, include the Presidential Unit Citation with 2 OLC, Air Force Commendation Medal, American Campaign Medal, American Defense Service Medal, Asiatic-Pacific Campaign Medal, Armed Forces Reserve Medal, and the WWII Victory Medal. Entering the civil service in January 1963, he began working for the Air Force on the SR-71 program at Norton AFB in California. After being employed in administration, security, and financial areas, Roger retired in January 1975.

Roger is married to the former Olga Irvin of Hurstville, Sydney, Australia. They have four children and five grandchildren. He is the older brother of Hector Devargas (see page 59).

---

1. All photos courtesy of Roger Vargas

STAFF SERGEANT
RAUL VASQUEZ

TUCSON

Army Air Corps
Gunner on B-24H
579th Bomb Squadron, 392nd Bomb Group
European Theater, 8th Air Force

Sgt. Raul Vasquez, tail gunner on a B-24 Liberator, was KIA on a mission to Kiel, Germany, January 4, 1944. The tail gunner on another plane reported "Ship sighted going down in flames after fighter attack from rear made thru vapor trail. Three chutes seen near Heligoland". There were no survivors.[1]

---

1. Missing Aircrew Report #1911, National Archives, Suitland, Maryland.

ARM1c
JOHN L. VILLARREAL

US Navy

Entered Service December 1940
Radioman/Gunner on SBD Dauntless
Bombing Squadron VB-6, Flight 300 (Guadalcanal), Air Group 5
Pacific Theater aboard USS Enterprise and USS Yorktown
Two Distinguished Flying Crosses, seven Air Medals, Purple Heart

---

While John was visiting his parents in Phoenix, the following news item appeared in the Arizona Republic on December 6, 1942.

Because of wartime conditions in 1942, the Arizona Republic was not allowed to print the name of John's aircraft carrier, which was the USS Enterprise. As a rear seat gunner on a Douglas Dauntless dive-bomber, flying off this carrier and later from Henderson Field on Guadalcanal, he experienced considerable action during his first tour of the war. Two books describing the events and conditions he and his fellow warriors endured while defending Guadalcanal are *The Cactus Airforce*, by Thomas G. Miller and *Dauntless Helldivers*, by Harold L. Buell.

Arizona governor Sidney Osborn, upon reading the above Arizona Republic news article, sent John the following letter:[1]

---

1. Letter courtesy of Linda Coe

ARM1c JOHN L. VILLARREAL

SIDNEY P. OSBORN
GOVERNOR

Executive Office
State House
Phoenix, Arizona

December
Eighth
1942

Mr. John L. Villarreal
243 East Monroe Street
Phoenix, Arizona

My dear Mr. Villarreal:

I read with interest the account of your experiences in the Pacific War Zone, that was published in the Republic.

It is on men like yourself that we who are behind the lines must depend for protection. We will try to do our part by backing you up with the essential tools and equipment for fighting.

I hope that you will enjoy your leave with your parents to the full and that good luck will continue to be your companion.

Sincerely,

SPO:v

After a much-deserved period of rest and recuperation, John returned to the Pacific and continued flying combat missions as an aerial gunner with Bombing Squadron Six (VB-6) aboard the USS Enterprise, and later with Air Group Five (AG-5) aboard the USS Yorktown. On April 29, 1944, while serving with Task Force 58, he was wounded on a mission to bomb the Japanese stronghold at Truk. Returning to the States, John spent the remainder of the war as an instructor at various training facilities.

ARM1c John Villarreal (Second from left) with fellow squadron mates somewhere in the Pacific. (Official US Navy photograph)

Remaining in the service for an additional sixteen years after the war ended, John rose to the rank of chief petty officer. During the later stages of his Navy career, he wrote and produced shows for public television, and technical films for closed circuit TV. In the early 1960s, while still in his 30s, John retired from the Navy with 21 years of service. His decorations include two Distinguished Flying Crosses, seven Air Medals, Purple Heart, Presidential Unit Citations, six Good Conduct Medals, American Defense Service Medal with Fleet Clasp, National Defense Service Medal, WWII Victory Medal, American Area Asiatic Pacific Medal with nine stars, and American Campaign Medal.

Fluent in Spanish and armed with communication skills he had acquired in the Navy, Mr. Villarreal returned to civilian life destined for bigger challenges. He produced, directed, and hosted a weekly bilingual television show at KOVR channel 13 in Sacramento, California, and in 1974 he moved to Washington, D.C., where he was a communications and ethnic minority specialist with the Department of Commerce and the Navy. In January 1980, John was named vice president of community relations and a member of the board of directors of Sacramento Cablevision Inc. He was part of a group seeking the Sacramento franchise for cable television. Unfortunately, he never realized this dream. He suffered a heart attack and died in February, 1980. He was 56 years old, married and the father of six children.[2]

---

2. Note: In the early stages of research for this book, my primary sources for finding names of Hispanic airmen were the wartime (1941-1945) newspapers from various cities and towns throughout Arizona. Upon reading the Arizona Republic article shown above, I began a search to find John Villarreal or members of his family. Repeated attempts over several years were unsuccessful. Finally, I was able to locate two of his former Flight 300 squadron mates, Harold L. Buell and Stuart James Mason, which resulted in my contacting John's sister, Linda Coe, in California. Being the family historian, she was able to provide me with the information necessary to complete the story.

   As it turns out, at the time of the Arizona Republic article, John was visiting his parents, Pedro and Irene Villarreal, who were living in Phoenix where Pedro worked for Safeway supermarket. John never lived in Arizona. He was born in San Antonio, Texas, and raised in East Los Angeles. He joined the Navy at 17 in Los Angeles and proceeded to the Naval Air Station in San Diego for training.

   I have shamelessly violated the premise of this book to feature only boys from Arizona. I feel justified to include John because of the extraordinary feats of this young man. It's a story that could not go untold.

   I am not related to John, at least not for three generations back. I find it exciting though, that John's father, Pedro Villarreal and my grandfather Rosendo Villarreal are from Monterrey in Mexico. Whether we are distantly related, I will leave to the genealogists to determine.

STAFF SERGEANT
JOE YANEZ

NOGALES

Army Air Corps
Entered Service January 1942
Gunner on B-17G
710th Bomb Squadron, 447th Bomb Group
European Theater, 8th Air Force
Air Medal with OLC

On March 3, 1944, Sgt. Yanez, waist gunner on a B-17 Flying Fortress, was killed when his plane went down in the North Sea. He had flown over 10 missions, and was returning to his base at Rattlesden, England, after a bombing mission to Berlin.[1]

---

1. Missing Aircrew Report #4436, National Archives, Suitland, Maryland.

Joe Yanez Missing

Nogales Air Gunner Lost In Raid Over German Held Territory

Staff Sgt. Joe Yanez, 23, son of Mrs. Hortensia P. Yanez of 125 Walnut Street, has been missing in action over Germany since March 3, according to a War Department message received yesterday evening by the family.

Sgt. Yanez, a waist gunner on an Eighth Air Force Flying Fortress, only recently had been mentioned in an AAF press release from England crediting him with destruction of a German plane in a raid over Brunswick.

It was a bigger raid, however, that probably ended the flying career of the young Nogalian. On reports Sgt. Yanez as missing, the date that the War Department Associated Press files disclose that a large force of American heavy bombers reached and bombed the outskirts of Berlin. Many of the American planes were forced down in German territory and among them, it is believed, was Sgt. Yanez.

Former Bank Employe

A 1938 graduate of Nogales High School, Sgt. Yanez was employed by the First National Bank prior to departure for service. He visited Nogales in October on furlough. His elder brother, Ramon, is with the U.S. Marine Corps at San Diego.

Sgt. Yanez was credited with destroying an ME 109 in the Brunswick raid.

"I never saw so many fighters in all my nine missions," Sgt. Yanez reported at the time.

Yanez is the third Nogales gunner downed over Europe. The other two are James and George Mabante. The latter was reported a prisoner of Germany, but no word has been received regarding James.

JOE YANEZ

This article appeared in the Nogales Herald on March 18, 1944.

APPENDIX A

ACRONYMS AND ABBREVIATIONS

AAC	Army Air Corps
AF	Air Force
AM	Air Medal
AMM2c	Aviation Machinist Mate second class
AMM3c	Aviation Machinist Mate third class
ARM1c	Aviation Radioman first class
ARM2c	Aviation Radioman second class
Bomb/Nav	Bombardier Navigator
Capt	Captain
CBI	China Burma India (Theater of Operations)
Cpl	Corporal
DFC	Distinguished Flying Cross
DNB	Death non-battle
DSC	Distinguished Service Cross
ENS	Ensign
ETO	European Theater of Operations
FE	Flight Engineer
FO	Flight Officer
FOD	Finding of Death
KIA	Killed In Action
Lt	Lieutenant
1st Lt	First Lieutenant

2nd Lt	Second Lieutenant
MIA	Missing In Action
MOS	Military Occupational Specialty
MTO	Mediterranean Theater of Operations
NATS	Naval Air Transport Service
OLC	Oak Leaf Cluster
PH	Purple Heart
POW	Prisoner Of War
PTO	Pacific Theater of Operations
RO	Radio Operator
Sgt	Sergeant
S/Sgt	Staff Sergeant
T/Sgt	Technical Sergeant
UNK	Unknown
USCG	United States Coast Guard
USMC	United States Marine Corps
USN	United States Navy
WO	Warrant Officer

APPENDIX B

FLYBOY LIST

Refer to Acronyms and Abbreviations on Page 231

RANK	NAME	SERVICE	HOMETOWN	MOS	COMMENTS
S/Sgt	Ernest P. Abril	AAC	Tucson	Gunner	See Text
S/Sgt	Norman F. Acido	AAC	Nogales	Gunner	See Text, KIA
Unk	Jesus G. Aguilar	AAC	Aguila	RO/Gunner	
1st Lt	Manuel Aguirre	AAC	Morenci	Bombardier	See Text
Unk	Mark Aguirre	AAC	Morenci	Pilot	DNB
S/Sgt	Ernest T. Alvarez	AAC	Unk	Gunner	See Text, MIA, FOD
T/Sgt	Guillermo V. Alvillar	AAC	Clarksdale	RO/Gunner	AM, ETO
2nd Lt	Frank R. Amado	AAC	Nogales	Pilot	
S/Sgt	Robert Aquilas	AAC	Superior	Gunner	9th AF
Sgt	Lucio Archuleta	AAC	Miami	FE/Gunner	
Sgt	Concepcion V. Armenta	AAC	Tucson	Gunner	

S/Sgt	Johnny V. Armenta	AAC	Tucson	Gunner	AM, 8th AF
S/Sgt	Raul Arrendondo	AAC	Douglas/ Tucson	RO/Gunner	AM, ETO
S/Sgt	David S. Avilla	AAC	Phoenix	Gunner	See Text
S/Sgt	Robert S. Baca	AAC	Globe	Gunner	AM, PH, ETO, POW,
T/Sgt	Jesus A. Balderrama	AAC	Phoenix	FE/Gunner	AM, 8th AF
2nd Lt	Apolonio "Hap" Barraza	AAC	Tolleson	Navigator	See Text
S/Sgt	Fernando "Fritz" Belis	AAC	Tucson	Gunner	See Text, KIA
2nd Lt	Roger Benavidez	AAC	Morenci	Bombardier	DFC, AM, 8th AF
S/Sgt	Amado Berrellez	AAC	Nogales	Gunner	See Text
T/Sgt	Jose Berrellez	AAC	Nogales	RO/Gunner	AM, PTO
Sgt	Joseph G. Bernal	AAC	Tucson	Gunner	
T/Sgt	Raymond Bernal	AAC	Tucson	FE/Gunner	See Text
Sgt	Edmundo L. Blanco	AAC	Benson	Unk	AM, PTO
S/Sgt	Inocente R. Boltarez	AAC	Hayden	Gunner	See Text, KIA
ARM 3c	Martin N. Cabral	USN	Clifton	RO/Gunner	DNB
Sgt	Eli Camacho	AAC	Prescott	FE/Gunner	9th AF

S/Sgt	Epifanio P. Campos	AAC	Safford	FE/Gunner	See Text
Lt	Manuel L Carrasco	AAC	Globe	Bomb/Nav	
S/Sgt	Servando Carrillo	AAC	Superior	RO/Gunner	See Text
S/Sgt	Louis D. Castellano	AAC	Nogales	RO/Gunner	AM, 8th AF
Lt	Ignacio "Nash" Castro	USN	Nogales	Pilot	See Text
Capt	Michael Castro	AAC	Phoenix	Bombardier	ETO
AMM 3c	Bob Cazares	USCG	Clifton	Gunner	
S/Sgt	Victor V. Cervantez	AAC	Morenci	Gunner	See Text
Cpl	Peter R. Chacon	AAC	Phoenix	Gunner	
S/Sgt	Frank F. Chavez	AAC	Casa Grande	Gunner	AM, 15th AF
Lt	Sam Cisneros	AAC	Nogales	Pilot	
Sgt	Manuel Cocio	AAC	Tucson	FE/Gunner	
T/Sgt	Francisco J. Colunga	AAC	Nogales	RO/Gunner	See Text, KIA
Sgt	Gustavo Contreras	AAC	Tucson	Gunner	See Text, KIA
T/Sgt	Anastacio Contreras	AAC	Morenci	RO/Gunner	DSC, PH
Capt	Luis B. Coppola	AAC	Nogales/ Tucson	Pilot	See Text

Lt	Valdemar Cordova	AAC	Phoenix	Pilot	See Text, POW
Sgt	Edward Corona	AAC	Yuma	Unk	ATC, CBI
S/Sgt	Gilbert S. Corona	AAC	Yuma	RO/Gunner	See Text, POW
1st Lt	Vidal J. Cortez	AAC	Mesa	Pilot	See Text
Sgt	Cecilio De Jesus	AAC	Clifton	Gunner	AM, PTO
2nd Lt	Jesus De La Garza	AAC	Douglas	Pilot	AM, ETO
Lt	John A. De Gomez	USN	Bisbee	Pilot	
Lt	Jerry Delgado	AAC	Tucson	Pilot	AM, PH, ETO
2nd Lt	Hector E. DeVargas	AAC	Morenci	Bombardier	See Text, KIA
FO	Benjamin Diaz	AAC	Phoenix	FE	See Text
Capt	Joe Diaz	AAC	Tucson	Pilot	AM, PTO
S/Sgt	Julio R. Diaz	AAC	Phoenix	Gunner	See Text
Capt	Joseph S. Dominguez	AAC	Naco	Pilot	See Text
Sgt	William Encinas	AAC	Prescott	Gunner	ETO
Sgt	Louis S. Escobedo	AAC	Miami	Gunner	AM, 13th AF
S/Sgt	Joe T. Esparza	AAC	Phoenix	Gunner	AM, MTO
Sgt	Arthur R. Estrada	AAC	Phoenix	RO/Gunner	See Text, KIA

Sgt	Robert J. Fernandez	AAC	Miami	Gunner	ETO
FO	Robert Gallardo	AAC	Jerome	Bombardier	
Cpl	Oscar C. Gallegos	AAC	Phoenix	Gunner	See Text, POW
1st Lt	Edward A. Garcia	AAC	Morenci	Pilot	See Text
S/Sgt	Fidel V. Garcia	AAC	Hayden	RO/Gunner	AM, 15th AF
Capt	Robert M. Garcia	AAC	Tucson	Pilot	See Text
Lt	Gilbert W. Gomez	AAC	Yuma	Bombardier	MTO
T/Sgt	John V. Gomez	AAC	Phoenix	Gunner	AM, 8th AF
Lt	Tony D. Gomez	USN	Bisbee	Pilot	
1st Lt	Gilbert F. Gonzales	AAC	Tucson	Pilot	See Text
Capt	Louis R. Gonzales	AAC	Tucson	Glider Pilot	AM, ETO
Capt	Robert F. Griego	AAC	Flagstaff	Bombardier	
S/Sgt	Nicholas B. Guerra	AAC	Clifton	Gunner	See Text
FO	Baldo M. Hernandez	AAC	Miami	Bombardier	
S/Sgt	Enrique M. Huerta	AAC	Nogales	FE/Gunner	8th AF
S/Sgt	Alfred L. Huish	AAC	Douglas	Aerial Photo	See Text, POW

Lt	Heber M. Huish	AAC	Douglas	Pilot	See Text, KIA
Lt	Willardo Jaime	AAC	Williams	Pilot	
Lt	Salvador Jury	USMC	Nogales	Pilot	
S/Sgt	Charles G. Lama	AAC	Phoenix	RO	AM
S/Sgt	Manuel H. Larini	AAC	Ray/Sonora	Gunner	See Text, KIA
ARM 3c	Victor S. Leon	USN	Phoenix	Unk	
Sgt	Henry Leyva	AAC	Tucson	RO/Gunner	See Text
1st Lt	Orlando Loera	AAC	Mesa	Bombardier	See Text, KIA
Cpl	Nephi E. Lopez	AAC	Douglas	Gunner	
S/Sgt	Richard L. Lopez	AAC	Tucson	Gunner	AM, 8th AF
S/Sgt	Frank G. Mabante	AAC	Nogales	Gunner	See Text, POW
S/Sgt	James A. Mabante	AAC	Nogales	Gunner	See Text, KIA
FO	Juan Madero	AAC	Tucson	Pilot	See Text, DNB
ARM 2c	Albert E. Madrid	USN	Clifton	RO/Gunner	See Text
Lt	Robert L. Madrid	AAC	Prescott	Unk	MIA
Sgt	Manuel R. Maldonado	AAC	Tucson	FE/Gunner	7th AF
Sgt	Epifanio Manriquez	AAC	Clemenceau	FE/Gunner	9th AF
Unk	Honorato Manriquez	AAC	Clemenceau	Pilot	

WO	Eugene A. Marin	AAC	Winkleman	Navigator	See Text
S/Sgt	Rudolph F. Mariscal	AAC	Miami	Gunner	AM, 15th AF
Ens	Alfred C. Marquez	USN	Mammoth	Pilot	See Text
Sgt	Arthur S. Martinez	AAC	Mesa	Gunner	8th AF, MIA
Sgt	Augustin G. Martinez	AAC	Flagstaff	Gunner	
S/Sgt	Maclovio Martinez	AAC	Flagstaff	Gunner	AM, 5th AF
S/Sgt	Robert M. Martinez	AAC	Phoenix	Gunner	DFC, AM, PH, ETO
Unk	Joe V. Mendoza	USN	Mesa	Gunner	AM
FO	Raul C. Mendoza	AAC	Hayden	Bombardier	
1st Lt	Ralph L. Michelena	AAC	Solomon	Pilot	See Text
Cpl	Rudolph Michelena	AAC	Phoenix	Gunner	AM, MTO
Sgt	Santiago G. Miranda	AAC	Tucson	Gunner	
FO	Narcisco M. Monje	AAC	Douglas	Glider Pilot	AM, PH, ETO
T/Sgt	Ignacio D. Mora	AAC	Prescott	FE/Gunner	DFC, AM, 9th AF
Capt	Raymond N. Moraga	AAC	Tempe	Pilot	See Text, KIA
Lt	Raymond Morales	AAC	Phoenix	Pilot	See Text

S/Sgt	Humberto J. Moreno	AAC	Tombstone	Gunner	AM, ETO
T/Sgt	Charles P. Navarro	AAC	Phoenix	FE/Gunner	See Text, KIA
T/Sgt	Raul A. Negrette	AAC	Williams	RO/Gunner	See Text
S/Sgt	Manuel W. Nevares	AAC	Tucson	Gunner	See Text
Sgt	Salvador A. Ocon	AAC	Miami	Gunner	12th AF
S/Sgt	Frank M. Ochoa	AAC	Phoenix	Gunner	See Text, KIA
S/Sgt	John Ochoa	AAC	Bisbee	Gunner	DFC, AM, 8th AF
FO	Reyes L. Olachea	AAC	Tempe	Glider Pilot	See Text
S/Sgt	Rudy L. Olague	AAC	Ashfork/ Phx	RO/Gunner	See Text, KIA
T/Sgt	Gregorio Oliva	AAC	Winslow	RO/Gunner	See Text, POW
S/Sgt	Ramon B. Olivas	AAC	Nogales	Gunner	AM, 10th AF
1st Lt	Gilbert D. Orrantia	AAC	Clarkdale	Pilot	See Text
T/Sgt	Alfonso M. Ortega	AAC	Phoenix	Gunner	See Text
1st Lt	Jose V. Ortega Jr.	AAC	Tucson	Bombardier	See Text, KIA
S/Sgt	Joe B. Pacheco	AAC	Phoenix	Gunner	See Text, KIA
T/Sgt	Joseph M Pacheco	AAC	Phoenix	Unk	AM, ATC, CBI
Lt	Alexander B. Padilla	AAC	Nogales	Pilot	

S/Sgt	Moses D. Perales	AAC	Nogales	Gunner	AM, 8th AF
Sgt	William H. Perez	AAC	Globe	RO/Gunner	AM, ETO
Cpl	Richard S. Peyron	AAC	Tucson	Gunner	See Text, KIA
S/Sgt	Leo Picone	AAC	Miami	Unk	ETO, ATC
Cpl	Ignacio J. Pina	AAC	Nogales	Gunner	
S/Sgt	Joe D. Pulido	AAC	Tucson	Gunner	AM, 8th AF
Lt	AL D. Quinones	AAC	Mesa	Pilot	See Text, POW
S/Sgt	Manuel A. Ramirez	AAC	Phoenix	Gunner	See Text, KIA
T/Sgt	Walter F. Ramirez	AAC	Nogales	RO/Gunner	ETO, POW
S/Sgt	Manuel M. Ramos	AAC	Douglas	RO/Gunner	See Text, KIA
S/Sgt	Julian G. Renteria	AAC	Miami	Gunner	AM, 15th AF
FO	Arthur Reade	AAC	Globe	Pilot	AM, CBI, ATC
Sgt	Miguel A. Reyes	AAC	Tucson	Gunner	See Text, KIA
AMM 2c	Everardo R. Reynoso	USN	Ray/Sonora	FE/Gunner	See Text
S/Sgt	Louis R. Rivas	AAC	Phoenix	Gunner	AM, 13th AF
Lt	Raymond L Robles	AAC	Phoenix	Pilot	10th AF
S/Sgt	Ernesto Rodriquez	AAC	Bisbee	Gunner	DFC, AM, ETO

S/Sgt	Ramon C. Rodriguez	AAC	Tucson	Gunner	DFC, AM, 8th AF
FO	Fernando A. Romero	AAC	Tucson	Unk	20th AF, PTO
Sgt	James R. Ruiz Jr	AAC	Superior/ Mesa	Gunner	DNB
S/Sgt	Joe P. Ruiz	AAC	Phoenix	Gunner	See Text, DNB
S/Sgt	Ed Saavedra	AAC	Jerome	Unk	AM, ETO
Sgt	Guillermo F. Salas	AAC	Ray/Sonora	Gunner	14th AF, CBI
Sgt	Jesus M. Salas	AAC	Globe	Gunner	See Text, KIA
S/Sgt	Albert M. Salazar	AAC	Phoenix	Gunner	See Text, KIA
S/Sgt	Anthony Sanchez	AAC	Tucson	Gunner	
S/Sgt	Frank Sanchez	AAC	St. John	RO/Gunner	AM, PH, 8th AF
S/Sgt	Joseph A. Sanchez	AAC	Superior	Gunner	
S/Sgt	Julio Sanchez	AAC	Clarksdale	Gunner	DFC, AM, ETO
T/Sgt	Robert L. Sanchez	AAC	Winslow	RO/Gunner	See Text, POW
1st Lt	Hector J. Santa Anna	AAC	Miami	Pilot	See Text
Sgt	Fred C. Saucedo	AAC	Unk	Gunner	See Text, KIA
1st Lt	Miguel M. Serna	AAC	Ray/Sonora	Bombardier	See Text
Sgt	Rudolph M. Silva	USMC	Bisbee	Gunner	

Rank	Name	Branch	Hometown	Role	Notes
Lt	Robert S. Sosa	AAC	Douglas	Navigator	See Text, KIA
FO	Marcello H. Soto	AAC	Miami	Bombardier	
Capt	Oscar C. Soto	AAC	Nogales	Pilot	See Text
T/Sgt	Roman S. Soto	AAC	Soloman	RO/Gunner	DFC, AM, ETO
S/Sgt	Charles M. Sotelo	AAC	Bisbee	Gunner	See Text, KIA
ARM 3c	R. O. Tellez	USN	Clifton	RO/Gunner	PTO
Lt	Walter M. Tellez	AAC	Tucson	Pilot	
1st Lt	Manuel Trevino Jr	AAC	Superior	Pilot	See Text
T/Sgt	John R. Trujillo	AAC	Ray/Sonora	FE/Gunner	See Text, MIA
Unk	Ferdinand R. Urbino	AAC	Nogales	Pilot	
ARM 3c	Tony Uribe	USN	Nogales	RO/Gunner	
Unk	Andres Valdez	AAC	Douglas	Bombardier	CBI
Sgt	Raul J. Valenzuela	AAC	Phoenix	Gunner	DNB
Capt	Roger E. Vargas	AAC	Morenci	Navigator	See Text
FO	Robert H. Vasquez	AAC	Tucson	Bombardier	
S/Sgt	Guillermo A. Vasquez	AAC	Tucson	Gunner	AM, 8th AF
S/Sgt	Raul Vasquez	AAC	Tucson	Gunner	See Text, KIA

Sgt	William G. Vasquez	AAC	Tucson	RO/Gunner	15th AF
T/Sgt	Joe R. Vega	AAC	Tucson	RO/Gunner	DFC, AM, 8th AF
Sgt	Robert S. Vergara	AAC	Tucson	Gunner	
S/Sgt	Arturo C. Villa	AAC	Nogales	Gunner	AM, 15th AF
ARM 2c	John L. Villarreal	USN	Los Angeles	RO/Gunner	See Text
Sgt	Ignacio Vindiola	AAC	Douglas	RO	PTO
S/Sgt	Joe Yanez	AAC	Nogales	Gunner	See Text, KIA

Bibliography

BOOKS AND PERIODICALS

Ambrose, Stephen E., *Citizen Soldiers*, Simon & Schuster, New York, 1997.

Ambrose, Stephen E., *D-Day*, Simon & Schuster, New York, 1994.

Birdsall, Steve, *Flying Buccaneers*, Doubleday, Garden City, NY, 1977.

Buell, Harold L., *Dauntless Helldivers*, Orion Books, New York, 1991.

Cales, James H., *Rememberances of Guadalcanal*, THE HOOK magazine, August, 1990.

Coffey, Thomas M., *Decision Over Schweinfurt*, David McKay Company, New York, 1977.

Comer, John, *Combat Crew*, William Morrow, New York, 1988.

Cressman, Robert J., & Wenger, Michael J., *Steady Nerves And Stout Hearts,* Pictorial Histories Publishing, Missoula, Montana, 1990.

Crews, Howard W., with Buell, Harold L., *VF-5 and the Cactus Air Force*, THE HOOK magazine, August, 1990.

Ford, Daniel, *Did He Say Five Hundred Feet?*, Air & Space magazine, June/July 1994.

Freeman, Roger A., *Zemke's Wolf Pack*, Orion Books, New York, 1988.

Kepchia, John B., *M.I.A. Over Rabaul*, The Palace Printer, 1986.

Kuhl, George C., *Wrong Place! Wrong Time!*, Schiffer Publishing, Atglen, Pa., 1993.

Lawson, Capt. Ted W., *Thirty Seconds Over Tokyo*, Random House, New York, 1943.

Marrin, Albert, *The Airman's War*, Antheneum, New York, 1982.

Marshall, Bill, *Angeles Bulldogs & Dragons*, Champlin Museum Press, Mesa, Arizona, 1984.

Miller, Thomas G., *The Cactus Air Force*, Harper & Row, New york, 1969.

Morin, Raul, *Among The Valiant*, Borden Publishing Co. Los Angeles, Ca. 1963.

Olynyk, Frank J., *USAAF (European Theater) Credits For The Destruction Of Enemy Aircraft In Air-To-Air Combat World War 2*, Frank J. Olynyk, 1987.

Olynyk, Frank J., *USAAF (Mediterranean Theater) Credits For The Destruction Of Enemy Aircraft In Air-To-Air Combat World War 2*, Frank J. Olynyk, 1987.

Sides, Hampton, *Ghost Soldiers,* Doubleday, New York, 2001.

Stafford, Edward P., *The Big E*, Random House, New York, 1962.

Steinbeck, John, *Bombs Away*, Paragon House, New York, 1942.

Sulzberger, C. L., *World War II,* American Heritage Publishing, 1966.

Taylor, Michael J. H., *Jane's Encyclopedia Of Aviation*, Portland House, New York, 1989.

The Honor List Of Dead And Missing For The State Of Arizona, US War Department, January, 1946.

The Sahuaro, Arizona State College at Tempe yearbook, 1940.

The Superstition, Mesa High School yearbook, 1937.

The World At Arms, The Reader's Digest Illustrated History Of World War II, Reader's Digest, 1989.

Wible, John T., *The Yamamoto Mission*, The Admiral Nimitz Foundation, 1988.

NEWSPAPERS

Arizona Blade Tribune, Florence, Arizona

Arizona Daily Star, Tucson, Arizona

Arizona Record, Globe, Arizona

Arizona Rebublic, Phoenix, Arizona

Arizona Silver Belt, Miami, Arizona

Bisbee Daily Review, Bisbee, Arizona

Coconino Sun, Flagstaff, Arizona

Douglas Daily Dispatch, Douglas, Arizona

El Sol, Phoenix, Arizona

Graham County Guardian, Safford, Arizona

Mesa Journal Tribune, Mesa, Arizona

Nogales Herald, Nogales, Arizona

Phoenix Gazette, Phoenix, Arizona

Prescott Evening Courier, Prescott, Arizona

Southside Progress, Tempe, Arizona

St. Johns Herald Observer, St. Johns, Arizona

The Copper Era, Clifton, Arizona

Tempe Daily News, Tempe, Arizona

About the Author

Rudy Villarreal is a native of Morenci, Arizona. A graduate of Northrop Institute of Technology, he is retired after thirty years in the aerospace industry, having worked for Douglas, Lockheed, and Allied Signal. He served in the US Army from 1964 to 1966. Rudy and his wife Mary Ellen live in Tempe, Arizona.

COVER DESIGN

David Villarreal, nephew of the author, designed the book cover. He is a graduate of The Art Center Design College in Tucson, Arizona. Shown on the front cover are shoulder insignia for each Air Force unit in the US Army Air Corps during WWII.

0-595-25717-8